The Crisis in Middle Management

EMANUEL KAY

The Crisis in Middle Management

A Division of American Management Associations

Library of Congress Cataloging in Publication Data

Kay, Emanuel.
  The crisis in middle management.

  Includes bibliographical references.
  1. Middle managers—United States.   I. Title.
HF5500.3.U54K38   658.4'3   73-88963
ISBN 0-8144-5355-4

First printing

To Nordia, Carl, and Laurie

Preface

BACK IN THE LATE 1960s our manpower agendas gave great emphasis to the problems of managing youth and minorities, applying behavioral science methods in the blue collar workforce to increase productivity, and to identifying and developing young, high-potential individuals for managerial positions. Much of this interest was supported by behavioral science theory and methods which seemed to offer the promise of a new and more productive and satisfied workforce. This enthusiasm was also supported by a booming economy and unbounded optimism for future economic growth.

It was during this time period of the late 1960s that I first came into contact with large groups of middle managers in seminars dealing with motivational themes and the new workforce. It was in these seminars when I first began to hear middle managers say "What you're proposing is fine (and sometimes even exciting), but what about us?" The discussions of the question of "what about us?" quickly revealed quite a bit of discontent—much of it quite near the surface. What the middle managers in those seminars seemed to be saying was that they, too, would like to work in the motivational climate that we were proposing that they create for their subordinates. At the time, it did not seem credible that this group, who by all objective indicators had made it in our society, could be expressing such discontent. A cursory review of the management literature of this period (1969) supported my observations in the seminars. There indeed appeared to be something going on in the middle management ranks. It was these experiences that ultimately lead me to write this book about a small (4 to 5 percent) but significant segment of our workforce.

There were other sources of stimulation and encouragement along the way which have made this book a reality, and I would like to acknowledge them at this time. First, I would like to thank Ernie Miller of American Management Associations for his initial support and for providing me with early versions of AMA reports relevant to middle managers. Second, I would like to thank Jim O'Toole who directed the HEW *Work in America* project. My contribution became the basis for this book. And third, I would like to thank the many middle managers who attended my seminars both in the United States and in Europe for speaking up and sharing their thoughts with me about what was happening in the middle management ranks. Their personal insights were invaluable to me.

During the time that I was writing the book, I was assisted greatly by Brenda Caldwell in the typing of the manuscript. Near the end, she moved to Gorham, Maine, and insisted on completing the manuscript in her usual conscientious fashion. To Brenda I express my sincerest appreciation for her efforts. I also am indebted to Mary Louise Byrd of American Management Associations for her detailed and thoughtful editing of the original manuscript. And, finally, to the folks at home—Nordia, Carl, and Laurie—my deepest appreciation for tolerating the inevitable periods of distraction and seclusion that go with writing a book.

EMANUEL KAY
Marblehead, Massachusetts
January 3, 1974

Contents

chapter one

Who Are the Middle Managers?

*And it came to pass on the morrow, that Moses sat to judge the people:
and the people stood by Moses from the morning unto the evening.*

*And when Moses' father in law saw all that he did to the people, he
said, What is this thing that thou doest to the people? Why
sittest thou thyself alone, and all the people stand by thee
from morning unto even?*

*And Moses said unto his father in law, Because the people come
unto me to enquire of God:*

*When they have a matter, they come unto me; and I judge
between one and another, and I do make them know the statutes of
God, and his laws.*

*And Moses' father in law said unto him, The thing that thou doest
is not good.*

*Thou wilt surely wear away, both thou, and this people that is with
thee: for this thing is too heavy for thee; thou art not able
to perform it thyself alone.*

*Hearken now unto my voice, I will give thee counsel.... thou shalt
provide out of all the people able men, such as fear God, men of
truth, hating covetousness; and place such over them, to be captains
of thousands, and captains of hundreds, captains of fifties, and
captains of tens.*

*And let them judge the people at all seasons: and it shall be, that
every great matter they shall bring unto thee, but every small matter they
shall judge: so shall it be easier for thyself, and they shall bear the
burden with thee.*

*If thou shalt do this thing, and God command thee so, then thou shalt
be able to endure, and all this people shall also go to their place in
peace.*

*So Moses hearkened to the voice of his father in law, and did all
that he had said.*

*. And Moses chose able men out of all Israel, and made them
heads over the people, captains of thousands, captains of
hundreds, captains of fifties, and captains of tens.*

*And they judged the people at all seasons: the hard causes they
brought unto Moses, but every small matter they judged themselves.
   And Moses let his father in law depart; and he went his way
into his own land.*

EXODUS 18, 13–27

THERE WE HAVE IT—the first recorded statement in man's history by a "management consultant" on how to design an organization. This quotation presents very concisely the basic problem in organizing an effort for a large group of people: the need for a leader to share his workload with others. Also, it clearly demonstrates how and why middle management positions originate.

WHY MIDDLE MANAGEMENT?

Typically, as the organization gets larger and the top executive no longer feels he can cope effectively with all of the management work, he calls on others to help him. In relatively small entrepreneurial organizations the top executive uses members of management as direct appendages of himself. In other words, he does most of the thinking and directing and the management team carries out his intentions. We also find that the top executive will reserve for himself a particular functional area—usually the one in which he has greatest competence and most often the one that helped him to start the business. For example, if he were an outstanding salesman, he would retain this function, even beyond the point where it no longer makes sense to do so. Thus in its most elementary form, middle management is really an extension of top management. Middle management exists because top management cannot cope with the workload.

THE GROWTH OF MIDDLE MANAGEMENT

As a business grows, however, the situation becomes more complex, and we can see some significant changes in the basic role of middle management. There are three aspects of growth in an organization that affect the role of middle management. One is sheer numbers. As the number of employees increases, the problem of more supervision comes to the fore, and work group supervisors are appointed. Continued growth then results in managers managing supervisors, and we find ourselves in the middle management ranks. And a hierarchy of supervision and management is generated, based primarily on the need to control the activities of large numbers of employees.

A second aspect of growth relates to functions. Typically, the first organization an overburdened top executive will create is a basic business operating function, such as sales, manufacturing, or engineering, supplemented initially by a control function such as finance. These functional heads ultimately, if not initially, become the vice presidents; in turn, they, as the organization continues to grow, face the same problems as the top executive: how to manage an organization which is growing both in numbers and in subfunctional specialties.

Not too surprisingly, the future vice presidents react to this situation in the same way as the top executive did, by putting in a level or levels of management below themselves. (This really is how one gets to be a vice president—build an organization under yourself.) These subfunctional managers also become part of the middle management population.

A third result of growth occurs when an organization develops a large number of different products or services or when they start to serve the needs of different markets. At this point, we begin to see the development of self-contained product divisions; that is, these divisions have all the functions and resources they need to make and sell a product or to serve a market. These "businesses within a business" usually can operate autonomously as separate enterprises. Typically, they are constrained by the parent corporation in terms of capital investment, compensation and benefit systems, promotions above a certain level, use of the company logo, and financial reporting and controls.

The middle manager is now part of the ABC Division of the XYZ Corporation. He now must be responsive to the top management of ABC as well as to some of the organizational needs of XYZ and the constraints that are imposed by XYZ. Thus he finds himself, in effect, a member of two organizations—one nearby and one somewhat geographically distant.

MIDDLE MANAGEMENT'S RESPONSIBILITY

The process through which middle management evolved is referred to as *differentiation*. This term aptly describes the development of an organization: from a rather simple structure with some basic functions to greater numbers and greater specialization of work units and individuals. Differentiation creates the need for another process in the organization in which the middle managers play a key role: the process of *integration*. In many respects, a business organization can be thought of as a sequence of activities which have to be performed in a highly coordinated manner to achieve a profitable result. The need for integration and coordination is necessary at all levels in an organization, but is generally regarded as a prime function of middle management. They, in effect, operate the management system in its day-to-day aspects.

The integration responsibilities of middle managers take two forms. First, they integrate horizontally. For example, the manager of a machined parts operation has to dovetail the efforts of his organization with those of the manager of the assembly area or chaos results. In many organizations this horizontal integration is very complex and is supported by elaborate planning systems. Sometimes entire departments are devoted to horizontal integration, such as production control. Whatever form horizontal integration takes, it is a basic responsibility of middle managers.

Middle managers also integrate vertically. In most organizations the word presumably comes down from the top through channels and back up through the same channels. Middle managers, who occupy the organizational space between the top and the bottom echelons, are those channels through which information flows. From a top-down point of view, they are expected to interpret the intent of top management to the lower echelons. From a bottom-up point of view, they provide top management with information about the functioning of the organization.

Thus we begin to get our first focus on the origins of middle management and who the middle managers are. We can now proceed to define more formally the middle management population.

WHO ARE THE MIDDLE MANAGERS?

Most definitions of middle management identify them as being the managers between the first level of supervision and the top executives, that is, vice president.[1,2] This is a rough cut but reasonably accurate. Our definition of middle management will be somewhat more formal and consider in more detail the upper and lower cutoff limits for this group.

Basically, middle managers manage other managers and supervisors. In this role, they appear on organization charts as subfunctional heads, for example, manager, assembly operations; manager, engineering evaluation; manager, northeast region sales. In such professional organi-

[1]Peter M. Blau and Richard A. Schoenherr, *The Structure of Organizations.* New York: Basic Books, 1971.
[2]Lyman W. Porter and Richard E. Lawler III, *Managerial Attitudes and Performance.* Homewood, Ill.: Richard D. Irwin, 1968.

zations as engineering and information systems, the first-line supervisor who is supervising primarily exempt employees also should be included in the category of middle manager. First-line supervisors who primarily supervise nonexempt employees are excluded. This does not mean that their problems are not worthy of attention but that they do not come within the discussion of this book. Thus far, we have established the *lower limit* for inclusion in middle management.

In the same manner, we need to set an *upper limit* for inclusion in the middle management ranks. First, for the upper limit we exclude

- Heads of major functional areas (whether they are vice presidents or not) and heads of staff functions.
- Chairman of the board, president, executive vice president, and group vice president.
- Division general managers who have profit-and-loss responsibility for a segment of products or services. These positions may have the title of division president, division vice president, division president, or vice president of the corporation. The important distinction is the profit-and-loss responsibility.

These people above the upper limit are those who typically have a broader role and a more total view of the organization and its operations and objectives. Again, we exclude them from consideration not because they are not worthy of study but because they are beyond the scope of this book.

One word of caution in determining who the middle managers are has to do with position titles. Titles such as manager, vice president, general manager are not used uniformly among companies and in many cases there is less than desired uniformity within companies. Therefore they are a poor guide to job functions. At the upper limit, the key question to ask is, Does the incumbent manage a total major function? If the answer is yes, the individual is excluded. At the lower limit, the question is, Does the incumbent manage other managers, exempt professional or technical people, or some combination of the two? If the answer is no, he is excluded.

There also are some considerations in respect to middle managers in staff organizations. In some cases staff organizations have evolved from groups of specialists to quasi-production organizations. For example, as the needs for data processing have grown and high-capacity computers have become available, we find that systems and data processing work have been centralized and put into a staff organization such as finance. These moves have increased the stature of many finance organizations as well as given it the character of a production organization. In this case, the product is data output, but the division of labor in the data processing organization has resulted in an organization structure similar to those found in some manufacturing organizations. New management technology and growth in organizations is reducing the pure staff content in staff organizations, resulting in more production or operating type of work. The result is that they are acquiring a middle management structure similar to that in the operating functions.

HOW MANY MIDDLE MANAGERS ARE THERE?

To the best of my knowledge, there has not been a valid census made of the number of middle managers in different kinds of organizations using a standard definition. This would be a monumental undertaking, as the standard organization documents—organization charts, job titles, position descriptions, and so on—can only serve as rough guidelines. I was able to secure the cooperation of ten business organizations from the *Fortune* 500 directory to attempt a very crude census of middle managers using the definition proposed here. The surveyed companies are sprinkled throughout the *Fortune* 500 list but tend to dominate the middle third of the list. They represent aerospace (two), banking, retail sales, pharmaceuticals (two), insurance, electrical equipment manufacturing, and rubber products manufacturing. Analysis was made from organization charts and followed up by letters and phone calls to verify and clarify it.

Of all the individuals from the first level of supervision up through the chief executive officer, it was found that two-thirds to three-fourths of the supervisory, managerial, and executive population could be identified as middle managers. At first glance, this may seem to be surprising in that one might expect more first-line supervisors, in view of the downward pyramid effect, than middle managers. This would be so if there were just *one* level of middle management in the organization. Then we could expect the first-line supervisors to outnumber the middle managers by the multiple of the average span of control of the middle managers.

Two factors, however, explain this heavy concentration of middle managers. First, we found more than one level of middle management in each company and three or four levels in some! This multiplies the number of middle managers very rapidly. Second, we included as middle managers those who supervise exempt professional and technical employees, where this could be verified. This also tended to increase the number of middle managers. In effect, our definition of middle management limits the top management to two or three levels of management at most, with relatively small numbers and the first line to one level.

The major surprise, of course, was the number of levels occupied by middle managers. However, our findings are supported by Blau and Schoenherr's study[3] of the organization structure of state employment security offices. They found that the number of middle management levels increased as the size and number of functions in the organization increased. Apparently, with increased size come an increase in functional and subfunctional activities, a greater number of position titles in the entire organization, and a need for a middle management structure to manage and coordinate these activities. Our data, which hardly represent a scientific survey, suggest that two-thirds to three-fourths of the managerial population are middle managers engaged in these types of activities.

Next, we attempted to approximate the number of middle managers in the United States workforce. At this point, our results get decidedly cruder, but perhaps the attempt will stimulate more refined work in this area. In March 1972 (when the organization charts were analyzed) the Bureau of of Labor Statistics indicated 6.2 million individuals as salaried managers and administrators.[4] If we assume that two-thirds to three-fourths of these were middle managers, then we are talking about 4 to 4.5 million middle managers in the United States at that time. This works out to approximately 5 to 5.2 percent of the total nonagriculturally employed workforce (4 to 4.5 million middle managers in a workforce of 80.2 million).

From a *total* workforce point of view, the number of middle managers (assuming that the estimate is somewhere within reasonable bounds of accuracy) does not appear to be of significant size. Professional and technical employees constituted 14.0 percent of the workforce while the percentages for clerical, service workers (nonhousehold), and blue collar employees were 17.0, 34.4, and 11.6, respectively. Also, the managerial workforce has not grown at a faster rate than the total labor force since 1958, although other occupational groups, such as clerical, professional, and technical and service (nonhousehold), have grown at a significantly faster rate.[5,6]

[3]Blau and Schoenherr, op. cit.

[4]U.S. Bureau of Labor Statistics, *Employment and Earnings,* Vol. 11, No. 10, April 1972.

[5]U.S. Bureau of Labor Statistics, op. cit.

[6]U.S. Department of Labor, *Manpower Report of the President: 1971.*

Why then the concern with middle managers? The concern is not with the total size of the group but rather with what they do and where they are located in the hierarchy. Keep in mind that as organizations have grown and differentiated, the middle managers are the ones who have occupied the organizational space between the top and lower echelons. They, in effect, are the funnel through which the intentions of top management flow down and through which information about the organization flows up. The middle managers also are the integrators; they operate the management systems which make the organization work. The impact of this 5 percent is multiplied, for better or worse, on the other 95 percent (and this includes the one percent of the organization which is top management). If we can provide an environment in which our middle managers are more effective, then we can multiply the effectiveness of the entire organization. And, really, this is what this book is about.

chapter two

Perceived Problems
of Middle Managers

STARTING IN THE LATE 1960s, we began to get our first indications of
dissatisfaction in the middle management ranks. This was a period of
great exuberance and optimism in our economy, so one may wonder
why the problems of this group should start to surface at this time.
In retrospect, there appeared to be some major forces operating in our
society and business organizations which came together at the same
time to produce this situation.

WHY DISSATISFACTION?

The first factor to consider is the age distribution of the middle managers.
As can be seen from Figure 1, the largest group of middle managers
is in the 40 to 49 age range. This group essentially represents the first
post-World War II generation to achieve middle management status.
They came into industry, in all probability, in the early to mid-1950s
and represent a solid core of 20-year veterans. They have been exposed
to the realities of organization life long enough to recognize and to have
been affected by some of the negative aspects. Among these negative
aspects, which will be discussed in this chapter, are a leveling off in
the rate of salary growth, limited promotion opportunities, and a lack
of real authority in their organizations.

A second factor is the economic climate that existed in our economy
in the late 1960s. The sales and profit projections were highly optimistic
(beyond reason, at times, as it turned out), and there appeared to be
no limits to our growth. The question at this point was, Were the middle
managers getting their fair share of this growth in terms of compensation
and promotions? It would appear that they were not. Blue collar salaries

1.　Age distribution of 536 middle managers responding to AMA survey.

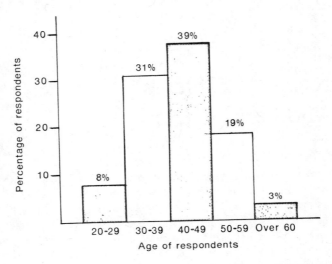

SOURCE: Alfred T. DeMaria, Dale Tarnowieski, and Richard Gurman, **Manager Unions?** AMA Research Report, 1972.

took off in the late 1960s and individuals in the public sector in comparable positions closed the gap in respect to compensation.

This also was a time of intense competition with the new college graduate, resulting in a faster rise in the starting rate for the new graduate as compared to the salary increases for those already on the payroll. Manager development programs under the general heading of early identification of management potential began to proliferate, which suggested that top management was placing its bets on the younger employee—one implication being that there was not much talent in the current middle management ranks worth developing.

The late 1960s was also a time when it became more socially acceptable to dissent. We saw it on the campuses, in the ghettos, and among consumers. As we look at the ways in which dissension was expressed, we see some interesting patterns. First, it was expressed by various groups, for example, students and blacks, who wanted to bring widespread attention to their concerns. Second, very strong tactics were used to bring the grievances to the attention of persons in authority. In the process, many of our traditional norms relating to authority were completely shattered, as many a university president can attest to.

The point is that we were in a period when certain groups could use what appeared to many to be outrageous tactics to bring about change. More important is that, to varying degrees, these tactics worked; they did result in some degree of change. Of course, we have never seen a middle management group take over the corporate president's office, but we have created a climate in our society where it is "more O.K." to speak up and speak out and expect some change as a result. After all, if the middle managers' children can do it, why shouldn't they?

And, of course, the final background factor we must consider is the 1970–1971 recession. The high expectations of the late 1960s vanished overnight, and many middle managers, for the first time in their working careers, experienced the problems of prolonged unemployment.

It is within this context that we examine the perceived problems of the middle managers. What problems do they see? What problems do the top executives see? And what problems do persons elsewhere in the hierarchy see?

The data sources describing middle manager problems are varied. First, a number of articles appeared in the management literature[1-6] dealing with such problems as lack of authority, obsolescence, job-hopping, insecurity, pay inequities, and the like. These articles typically reflected conditions in a particular business organization. The second source is a survey of 536 middle managers conducted by the American Management Associations.[7] As part of the survey, the managers were asked to select from a list of 19 conditions the three that, in their own estimate, would most likely produce middle management discontent with and alienation from top management. The survey also dealt with the issue of manager unions, which we will go into in more depth in Chapter 4. A third source of data is my personal experiences in consulting work with middle managers in many organizations in the private and public sectors in the United States and Europe. Combined, these data sources are far from complete and should not be construed as being a systematic analysis of middle management. Some caution should be exercised in making any generalizations.

[1]"The Revolt of the Middle Managers," *Dun's Review* (September 1969).

[2]"Young Managers Want Share of Power," *Employee Relations Bulletin* (November 25, 1970).

[3]"Executives in Ferment," *Dun's Review* (January 1971).

[4]"Managers Militant... Revolt or a Bill of Rights? *Industry Week* (March 22, 1971).

[5]Roger D'Aprix, "Coping with Company Power," *Industry Week* (May 31, 1971).

[6]William J. Constandse, "A Neglected Personnel Problem," *Personnel Journal* (February 1972).

[7]Alfred T. DeMaria, Dale Tarnowieski, and Richard Gurman, *Manager Unions?* AMA Research Report, 1972.

INEQUITABLE SALARY

Perhaps the bitterest complaint of middle managers has to do with inequitable salary treatment. This complaint generally revolves about what is called "the compression effect." The compression effect refers to the fact that the differential in salaries between longer-service and shorter-service employees is narrowing and has been narrowing over a period of many years. There are many reasons for this compression effect, but for middle managers two factors appear to contribute the most:

1. The individual's annual salary rate increase tends to be highest early in his career and then levels off for a number of years; in some cases it actually tapers off toward the end of his career. Thus, for the managerial population it is not uncommon to find that the annual rate of increase starts to level off at about age 35 or 40. What this means is that older employees get smaller percentage increases than newer employees and that the relatively larger percentages given to newer employees compress the differential between these two groups.

2. The starting salaries of new college graduates were going up at a significantly higher rate than the annual increases given to employees already on the payroll. These higher rates generally are attributed to the greater competition for the new college graduates.

The higher starting rate contributes to the compression effect in two ways. First, the increases themselves cause compression. Second, the higher starting rates are the base on which higher annual increases are given to a person early in his career. These two effects lead to a closing of the dollar gap between older and newer employees at a much faster rate.

The following data from one major industrial corporation illustrate the compression effect from the 1960–1970 period. For obvious reasons, this organization prefers to remain anonymous, although we can say it is within the top twenty of the *Fortune* 500 list and is large enough and diversified enough to be representative of American industry.

Years of Service	*Annual Rate of Salary Increase (%)*
20	3.3
15	3.7
10	4.2
5	4.4
1	4.8
0	5.6

As can be seen, the annual rate of salary increase is inversely related to years of service. The net result is that the actual salaries of newer people move closer to the salaries of longer-service people and the differential between the salaries of newer and older people continues to decrease over the years.

In its survey of middle managers AMA found that salary inequities were the most significant complaint of the middle managers, followed by concern about job security. As far as salary issues were concerned, middle managers not only cited the erosion of their position relative to new college graduates but also the relatively large and well-publicized increases received by union members during that time period.

From a motivation point of view, salary must be regarded as a "hygiene" factor. Hygiene factors are those issues that, if not satisfactory, have a marked propensity for producing discontent. In the case of the middle managers, the reported inequities in salary already seem to have caused considerable discontent. This is not too surprising in view of the circumstances of the time—the upsetting of traditional salary relationships by unusually large increases in the blue collar groups and the accelerating starting rates for new college graduates. Wage controls also had the effect of locking these inequities into place. In other words, there was not too much that management could do under the circumstances to correct the situation. The significant thing is that we now have a highly visible, emotional source of discontent among our middle managers. As we will see later, issues of this type can become a powerful rallying point for collective action on their part.

JOB INSECURITY

Pay problems were further aggravated by problems of job security. During the 1970–1971 recession the unemployment rate among middle managers went from slightly under 1 percent (1966–1969) to approximately 1.5 to 1.6 percent at the peak of the recession. The unemployment rates themselves are quite low, particularly when compared to that of the total workforce (5 to 6 percent). What is important is that the unemployment rate among middle managers increased very quickly by 50 to 60 percent and it occurred in a numerically stable group that traditionally had not experienced much unemployment.

The insecurity was also heightened by the publicity in the media regarding the length of time it took an unemployed manager to find another job. There are no statistics specific to middle managers on this subject, but there are statistics that generally support the notion that older people spend more time unemployed before they find their next job. To the extent that these statistics are representative of the total workforce, then, we can say that older middle managers have more difficulty in terms of time needed to get another position than younger middle managers.

The significant factor about the 1970–1971 recession in respect to middle managers is that they went from a traditionally low unemployment rate to a relatively higher one very suddenly. For the first time in many years, middle managers faced the loss of a job with a company. This experience and its attendant publicity in the media will be a source of continuing concern for years to come. It is grim evidence that they are not in a unique, favored, and protected position in the organization just because they are the echelon of management immediately below the top executives.

LACK OF AUTHORITY

Perhaps the first significant dimming of middle management status came when middle managers began to see how little authority and influence they had relative to top management. Middle managers could recommend and implement, but the power to decide remained in the hands of top management. How many times have you heard a middle manager say, "I have the responsibility but no authority." When you dig into this statement, you find that middle managers are referring to one or more of the following situations which militates against their authority.

Authority which is withheld explicitly. Most organizations have authorities which are withheld or which are given in amounts according to the person's position in the hierarchy. In policy manuals these restrictions usually come under the title of well-spelled-out approval authorities. For example, managers know that there are explicit limits to what they can approve in the way of capital expenditures. They may not like it and find ways to get around the restrictions; splitting the appropriation into two smaller amounts, each of which does not exceed their approval authority, is a popular, if obvious, method. Restrictions of this type, which are universal and generally have a sound business rationale, usually do not cause many problems. They may be annoying but they apply to everyone, and they do (or should) make good business sense.

Uncertain authority. The manager can find himself in a situation where he is uncertain of his authority or where conditions make him hesitant about using his authority. An example of the latter is the dismissal of a black employee for poor performance. The manager is convinced that the grounds for dismissal are sound and knows he has the authority to take the action. But what about the reaction to such a decision?

Will he be supported by the personnel department, for example? In some instances a manager may take some action in an uncertain or unfamiliar situation only to find later that the organization disapproved of what he has done, accompanied by some not too subtle hints not to do it again.

These uncertainties are very disturbing to managers in that they make them overly cautious or at times freeze them into very limited spheres of action. I recall one division sales manager who gave a discount to a customer in a situation where it made sense (to him) to do so. After the organization had made him appropriately aware of the error of his ways, he vowed never again to give a discount. Apparently, by his giving the discount, he created some problems with other customers. But no one had ever pointed this out to him.

Contingent authority. "I can't do anything until my boss makes a decision." How many times have you heard this one? Many a middle manager feels constrained to act until the word comes down from on high, and until such time, he waits. There are some subtler aspects to this situation. Not only must the middle manager wait until his boss makes up his mind but he must also wait for his boss to convince the top manager in *another* function. So the questions are, "When will he do it?" and even more important, "Will he be able to convince him?" In these respects, the middle manager's authority becomes contingent on his boss's timeliness and effectiveness.

The AMA survey of approximately 525 middle managers presents some data on the timing aspect of top management decisions. As can be seen from Table 1, approximately 50 percent of the middle managers in the age range of 20 to 59 see top management as "moderately slow" or "very slow" at reaching decisions. Top management may *not* be slow in making decisions, but the significant thing is that they are *seen* as being slow.

Extrafunctional authority. Middle managers also feel constrained in exerting authority or influence on managers in other functions. Perhaps an example would serve best to illustrate this situation.

Manager A heads a production unit. The product is relatively simple to make and the processes for making it are well established. The key to success in this operation is well-scheduled material input and keeping the work stations fully manned. Manager A is a no-nonsense type of person and tolerates very little in the way of absenteeism and tardiness, as a full staff and promptness are essential to his operation. His shop is unionized and he makes liberal use of the contract's discipline procedures in dealing with absenteeism and tardiness.

Across the street from Manager A's shop is the company R&D center. Casual observation of the R&D parking lot soon makes it clear that many of its employees come in late.

Table 1. How responding middle managers by age groups rate top management in their companies.

Description of Top Management	Percentage of Managers				
	Age 20 to 29	Age 30 to 39	Age 40 to 49	Age 50 to 59	Age Over 60
Highly innovative management, out-standingly open-minded	7	14	7	5	0
Reaches decisions and implements change with relative ease	10	17	12	14	50
Will entertain most suggestions for change, acts reasonably promptly	22	21	31	23	43
Moderately slow at reaching decisions, somewhat resistant to change	44	33	34	41	7
Very slow at reaching decisions, highly resistant to change	17	15	16	17	0

SOURCE: Alfred T. DeMaria, Dale Tarnowieski, and Richard Gurman, *Manager Unions?* AMA Research Report, 1972.

In a grievance session on a tardiness case, Manager A is told by the union that the company operates on a double standard—one for the shop operators and one for those people across the street. Manager A can deal with this situation; the contract applies to the shop personnel and not to the people across the street, but it is annoying and perhaps even embarrassing. So Manager A calls Manager B, the head of the R&D center, explains his problem and solicits his cooperation in getting the R&D people to arrive at work on time. Manager B listens attentively and points out that "we're different" and besides you and your people aren't around at night to see how many cars stay in the lot well after working hours. Sorry, but I've got the morale of my people to think of, and I can't regiment them to solve your problem. It would just create one for me and good scientists and engineers are hard to come by....

At this point, it would not be unreasonable for Manager A to say that he has the responsibility for operating a high-volume, low-cost shop, but that he lacks the authority to do so. What authority is he lacking? The authority to get Manager B to have his people come to work on time (which is a problem only to Manager A).

Just multiply this situation by the number of functions and middle management levels that exist in an organization, and the magnitude of the lack of influence which middle managers feel they have on each other becomes clear. This lack of lateral influence stems directly from the differentiation process. The different functions, in addition to developing unique work styles based on what they do and the types of employees they have, also tend to have stronger loyalties for what goes on within their own function as opposed to other functions. Thus the middle manager who is dependent on another function or being adversely affected by one may find that he has little direct authority to change situations to suit his needs.

In later chapters we will talk about some strategies and techniques for redistribution of authority between top and middle management as well as the interpersonal skill which can be taught to middle managers to help them in problem solving and conflict resolution among themselves.

CAREER INFLEXIBILITY

Another major concern of middle managers is their perceived loss of career flexibility. One of the prices paid for advancement in many organizations is the loss of opportunities to gain broadening career experiences. Early in one's career, there are many new things to learn and the loss of flexibility as a result of specialization is not felt. As an individual moves to a middle management position, the narrowness and specialization become more apparent, and he sees fewer lateral cross-functional or intra-functional experiences available to him. Five to seven years of work experience without one or two significant cross-functional experiences represents the threshold for producing another narrow middle manager. Beyond this point, it becomes increasingly difficult, if not impossible, to make any broadening moves.

Many middle managers feel that the management development system has boxed them in and they are being asked to pay the price for a situation that they did not create. And there is some support to their argument. For example, specialization starts in college when an individual elects a major subject. The typical college graduate will come into an organization through one of the major functions of the business—finance, sales, engineering, or personnel. Thus the specialization starts early in one's career and in effect becomes an extension of some choices that the individual made in college.

Once the person is in the organization, he is then subjected to additional factors which promote specialization. Jobs are designed to meet job evaluation and organization criteria, and technical rather than personal growth is emphasized. Also, ill-conceived and/or poorly executed development programs reinforce the resulting inflexibility. The result is narrowly defined jobs as well as relatively inflexible job boundaries. Not uncommonly, therefore, an individual goes along a narrow functional path and reaches a middle management position with little or no exposure to other business functions. The constraints on broadening him after he reaches middle management tend to be prohibitive. For example, a middle manager needing more exposure to and knowledge of a different function may not be moved to that function in a learning situation because of salary considerations. His salary is too high to justify a lateral move to another function.

OBSOLESCENCE

Inflexibility is also related to the middle manager's concerns with job insecurity. This insecurity is evident during favorable as well as unfavorable economic conditions. During favorable economic circumstances, the middle manager is concerned about the obsolescence of his skills rather than losing his job.

Most business organizations will tolerate a certain degree of obsolescence and attempt to deal with it in a way that is not too punishing for the individual. For example, the obsolescent manager may be assigned responsibilities in keeping with his perceived abilities, or he may be bypassed when new projects or new programs develop in the organization. In more extreme circumstances, early retirement may be encouraged. In general, the manager who is seen as obsolete will get indications that he is seen this way and he may experience some discomfort as a result. However, the economic consequences are not too severe if the organization decides to carry him in one capacity or another.

The notion of managerial obsolescence has become part of our management folklore. In fact, there is no hard evidence to support this notion, nor do we have a valid way of measuring obsolescence. The situation here is somewhat analogous to notions held, not too many years ago, about the length of careers for pilots. In this case the notion of pilot obsolescence was based on some erroneous assumptions that what it took to be a pilot—depth perception, good reflexes, aggressive attitudes, and so on—were characteristics of only younger men. We now know that flying depends on many skills and that accumulated experience, particularly as aircraft become more complex, more than compensates for any loss in physical attributes.

We tend to talk about managerial obsolescence in rather general terms. Cone [8, 9] has identified five aspects of managerial obsolescence:

Technological. Technological obsolescence occurs when the engineering manager has failed to keep up with the new developments in his field.

Interpersonal. This kind of obsolescence describes the manager who no longer possesses the interpersonal skills required for his present job. Thus an engineering manager may find that the interpersonal skills he used to supervise older engineers are not effective with a younger group.

Cultural. The cultural form is attributed to a manager who has certain cultural values that are in conflict with current cultural norms and values. For example, a manager may feel that employees should show a high degree of respect for persons in authority. This value runs counter to the attitudes of younger employees who are more open and equalitarian toward persons in authority. He may regard younger people as being disrespectful, and in this sense his attitude toward authority is culturally obsolete.

Political. A manager may be obsolete politically in terms of the internal politics of the organization. Over the years he may have been identified with a group which had power and influence but for various reasons has gone out of favor. To this extent, he also is out of favor and will be seen as lacking power and influence within the organization regardless of his ability.

Economic. An economically obsolescent manager is one whose aspirations for achievement do not meet those of the organization. Thus we might find an organization that is setting high goals for itself for what they consider to be good reasons. The economically obsolete manager does not identify with these goals or he considers them unrealistically high in the light of past levels of achievement expected from him. This manager would be seen as having lost his open drive and be either removed from his position or put aside.

[8]L. M. Cone, Jr., "Toward a Theory of Managerial Obsolescence: An Empirical and Theoretical Study," unpublished doctoral dissertation, New York University, 1968.

[9]L. M. Cone, Jr., "Society's Latest Disease—MO," *Marketing Review* (1969), pp. 15–17.

When a top manager says a middle manager is obsolete, he probably is referring to at least one or some combination of these five criteria. We have no hard data that would tell us how many middle managers fit the criteria and to what degree. The significant point about obsolescence is that the costs generated by this problem are hidden in that they cannot be measured in direct units of production. The effects of the obsolete manager are more nearly reflected in terms of poorly made decisions, poorly timed decisions, a lack of innovative or creative effort, and the resultant negative impact on the motivation and morale of the persons they supervise.

PERCEPTIONS OF MIDDLE MANAGERS

BY TOP MANAGEMENT

Top management is aware, or is becoming aware, of the rumblings in the middle management ranks. Their reactions, however—perhaps conditioned by the 1970–1971 recession—are not too favorable.

They are unrealistic about their environment. Top management tends to see middle managers as being unrealistic in their requests for facilities, personnel, and new or expanded programs. Not everyone can always get everything they want and middle managers should realize this when their requests are turned down (and not complain so much). Generally, middle managers are not aware of the factors against which their proposals are weighed. And that, of course, is the problem—they are left to their own devices to rationalize turndowns.

They are unrealistic about their roles. Top executives attach considerable importance to their own roles as decision makers, and they tend to strongly resist incursion by others on this prerogative. Top executives see middle managers as meddling in their decision-making role and at times feel they have to make it clear to middle managers "who makes decisions around here." There seems to be little sympathy to share decision-making powers with middle managers.

Top executives have been under increased pressure in recent years. Top executives are under considerable pressure to produce results for their organizations. They would like to enlist the aid of middle managers, and when they are unable to do so, they tend to become decidedly negative toward their middle managers. This negativism at times is reflected in an attitude of "if you don't like the way this company is run, then go elsewhere." While this is an understandable human reaction, the effect on middle managers can be quite significant. The better middle managers will in all probability take them up on their offer and leave, while those who remain will tend to withdraw, that is, take fewer risks and propose and push fewer ideas. In effect, a harsh take-it-or-leave-it attitude by top executives will tend to produce a more conforming and mediocre middle management.

They are obsolete, unambitious, and resistant to change. Another set of perceptions held by top executives about middle managers has to do with skills, ambition, and flexibility. In this case, top executives are reacting to symptoms (which in many cases are true) without fully understanding the reasons for the behavior. Quite frequently, top executives assume that the job performance of middle management is the result of poor selection. They then look to younger employees (who presumably were selected with "better" selection techniques) as their hope for the future. But what they fail to recognize and deal with is the fact that the systems for organizing, designing jobs, and developing people are at fault and tend to produce narrow, inflexible, and obsolete employees. They also fail to recognize that these systems, in time, will have the same effect on newer and younger employees.

In summary, the top executives appear to recognize the discontent in middle management and to recognize some of the symptoms. From what little evidence we have, however, it would appear that the top executives are reacting in an unproductive manner. They appear to be somewhat defensive about the middle managers and frustrated in their attempts to deal with them. There also appears to be a built-in conflict between the role of top executives and the role of middle managers, particularly relating to the sharing of authority. The role of top management traditionally has been one of decision making and policy making. There is little or no evidence at this point to indicate that top management is willing to share more of this influence with middle managers, which, in effect, is one of the key solutions to the problems facing middle managers.

BY SUBORDINATES

There is another set of perceptions of middle managers that not only affects them personally but also affects the significance and desirability of these jobs. This is the view that subordinates hold of middle managers. There are not even any soft data to support subordinate views of middle managers. What follows are my impressions based on experiences in a large number of business organizations over the last three years. These observations are included here because the subordinate perceptions are regarded as being quite important.

They have no influence. One perception of subordinates about middle managers is that they have little influence with top executives. Many of the requests that middle managers make of top management involve subordinates: pay increases, facilities, equipment, money for new programs, additional help, and so on. Subordinates can readily see the results of the manager's attempts to get approval from top management. Often, the middle manager is not even able to provide a good reason for the refusal because he has not been given one.

They are indecisive. Many middle managers give the impression of being indecisive because in fact they are not in a position to decide. The need to take decisions elsewhere for approval usually involves time and conveys the impression that the manager isn't capable of making up his mind. The need to plead the case at a higher echelon also gives organizations highly bureaucratic overtones with the middle managers seen as just one more cog.

They are inflexible. One of the key roles of the middle manager is being an implementor of organization policies and practices. At times, middle managers are put in a position of having to apply a policy or a practice that does not make much sense to subordinates. In these cases, loyal and conscientious middle managers will attempt to defend the policy and its application. This only serves to reinforce the subordinates' perception that the manager is inflexible and acting in a bureaucratic manner.

They have an undesirable job. Subordinates, particularly the more sophisticated, develop a fairly good perception of the middle manager's role and the bind he is in. What they see causes them to view the job as undesirable and not one to be aspired to. In effect, this can create a situation where less talented people are attracted to middle management jobs.

The above sounds very familiar. It has the ring of blue collar workers talking about the desirability of first-line supervisory jobs. Generally the foreman's job has been eroded to the point where it is no longer attractive (to competent people, that is) or viable. Is the same thing happening to the middle management job? Or has it already happened!

In this chapter a great deal has been said about the perceived problems of middle managers. They see themselves as having little influence on key policies and decisions in the organization; they are in a management system which causes them to become obsolete; they have received ample evidence in recent years that they are economically vulnerable in terms of holding their jobs; and they can point to data in their own organizations and in society at large that they are being treated inequitably from a salary point of view.

A few words are in order to put these findings into proper perspective. First, it should come as no surprise that the problems of salary inequity and job security are at the top of the list. After all, the available data were collected in a time (1971) when there were powerful and objective events in our society that supported these perceptions. Inflation, spiraling wage demands, and unemployment were major economic as well as political issues and received considerable attention in the mass media.

This does not mean that the salary and job security issues have always or will always be dominant. The importance attached to these issues will depend on the degrees of inequity and insecurity that people feel. If the inequity and insecurity issues were to be corrected, then we could reasonably expect them to drop to the bottom of the list in terms of importance to the middle managers. Whatever dissatisfaction they caused could be regarded as temporary. If these issues should persist, however, then we can expect a hardening of the negative attitudes and reactions of the middle managers to these issues.

The thing to remember about salary, in particular, is that it is the most objective measure an individual has of his worth to the organization. If the middle managers are chronically dissatisfied with their salary, and supported by objective data in their perceptions, then we run the risk of creating a chronically dissatisfied middle management. Salary is a very emotional issue, and if an individual is dissatisfied with his compensation relative to others, then we can expect this dissatisfaction to generalize and spread to other aspects of his work situation.

The problems of lack of authority and career inflexibility are more subjective and less objective data are available for comparison. Thus a middle manager may feel boxed in by the organization structure and promotion system, but he has no way of determining whether other middle managers feel the same and, if so, to what degree relative to himself. In addition, one does not become aware of these problems except over a long period of time. When a middle manager finally realizes that he lacks authority or that he is boxed in from a career point of view, a lot of time has gone by, and it may be too late for him to do much about the situation. He's pretty much trapped in the situation and, as we shall see in the next two chapters, he must find a way to adjust.

The point is that we must keep our perspective when dealing with the problems of middle managers. Issues of pay and job security are supported by a great deal of hard data and publicity in the media. They also can be very transient issues, and when they are corrected, we should not assume that the problems of middle managers have been solved. The chronic, less measurable, and more subjective problems of underutilization still remain.

chapter three

How Middle Managers Cope
as Individuals

LET US MAKE SOME assumptions: You are a middle manager of a subfunctional group. Four supervisors and two specialists report to you, and
your total operation consists of 54 people. You've just passed your for-
tieth birthday. I have arranged with the top management of your organization for you to remain in your present job for the *next twenty years.*
At age 60 you will be retired with appropriate ceremonies to enjoy your
well-earned pension. Remember, you will not move out of your present
job as long as you are with your organization.

Besides developing an intense dislike for me, what would you do?
How would you cope with this situation.?

Let me tell you how several hundred middle managers have responded
to this hypothetical situation. In approximate order of frequency of men-
tion, they replied,

1. Quit!
2. Look for fulfillment outside the job through hobbies, leisure-time
   activities, and professional and civic organizations.
3. Become indifferent to the situation and just do the best I can.
4. Build the size of my organization to challenge my interest and/or
   to protect my present position.
5. Would try it but probably couldn't put up with it for too long
   and would be forced to quit. Would consider changing careers
   if I couldn't find a better situation.
6. Would take technical and management courses to keep myself
   stimulated.
7. Can't accept your assumption. The organization is too dy
   namic and will have to change. I just can't believe that a situation like that could occur.

Of course, the situation I posed is not hypothetical, nor are the reactions. One of the realities of organization life for the middle manager is that he is destined to remain at the middle manager level for the remainder of his working career, regardless of the age at which he first became a middle manager. Twenty years is not unrealistic. If anything, it underestimates the time an individual might spend in this position if, for example, he became a middle manager at age 30 with retirement at age 60. The time one might spend in middle management is just one dimension of the problem. The other dimensions are why we get these reactions and how mature adults deal or cope with a situation of this type.

THE CAREER CRISIS

In order to understand these reactions we have to consider them in the broader context of a phenomenon referred to as the midcareer, or destination, crisis. Dr. Kenn Rogers, professor of business administration at Cleveland State University, describes the midcareer crisis:

> ... at some point between the ages of thirty and thirty-nine most people undergo a crisis in the course of which profound changes occur in the individual's relations to himself or herself and to his or her external environment. The feelings by American businessmen ... —frustration, anger, despair—are a typical outcry of persons caught up in what I call the mid-life crisis.[1]

Dr. Lee Stockford of Cal Tech conducted in-depth studies of 2,100 men and women. An examination of the case histories showed that 80 percent of executives age 34 to 42 are hit by a crisis that often results in intense personal discomfort and disturbed interpersonal relationships. Stockford sees the origins of the crisis in "the daily personal conflicts a young man undergoes when he finds his youthful ideals and goals banging up against business operations that seem to him low on principle and high on expedience."[2]

Dr. Daniel Levinson of Yale University refers to this time of life (age 39 and 42) as BOOM (becoming one's own man). This is a period marked by confusion and some intensive soul-searching about one's current relationships and career and what goals one is going to pursue for the remainder of one's life. The crisis seems to come whether one has

---

[1]Kenn Rogers, "The Mid-Career Crisis," *Saturday Review of the Society* (February 1973).
[2]Lee Stockford, in Kenn Rogers, op. cit.

been successful in one's work or not. It is not a reaction to failure. One significant point which Dr. Levinson makes is that the 40-year-old who makes a change, whether it be in his career, his marriage, or life-style, lives "in a state of suspended and breathless animation."[3] The point is that changes that are made at this time in life are complex and the outcomes—good or bad—are not immediately evident. In the meantime, one waits anxiously.

There appear to be two reactions to the midlife crisis. One is stagnation, which is characterized by surrender and passivity, that is, just accepting the crisis. The other reaction is coping, in which the individual meets the crisis head-on and tries to resolve the problems it raises for him. Why some individuals stagnate and others cope is not fully understood at this point. However, the reasons seem to be rooted in early childhood experiences, the effects of which resurface at this time of life. It would appear that the individual who goes the positive coping route is the one who maintains the vitality and zest to continue to develop in later adult stages.

In terms of this book, the midlife crisis has great significance in that it is indicative of a phase of life through which many middle managers are or shortly will be passing. In many respects it is like adolescence. We know it is a phase through which individuals pass and which has a great effect on them. We may not fully understand the effects of the midlife crisis, but we can anticipate that it is quite natural for middle managers to exhibit the behaviors associated with this developmental stage. We can no more deny the existence of a midlife crisis than we can adolescence.

If we now go back to the reactions to the hypothetical situation posed at the beginning of the chapter, we can interpret them in light of the midcareer crisis in the following way:

Reaction	*Midcareer Crisis Interpretation*
Quit	Positive coping reaction under the assumption that the individual is seeking a new job to satisfy new goals and interests.
Look for fulfillment outside the job through hobbies, leisure-time activities, professional and civic organizations.	Positive coping reaction as this involves an active search for fulfillment, albeit off the job.

[3]Linda Wolfe, "Behavior: A Time of Change," *New York* (June 5, 1972).

Become indifferent to the situation and just do the best I can.

Stagnation in its worst form.

Build the size of my organization to challenge my interests and/or to protect my present position.

Positive coping reaction if the individual is building his organization to challenge his interests. A stagnation reaction if the empire building is done solely for protection. Actually, it is probably a combination of both reactions.

Would try it but probably couldn't put up with it for too long and would be forced to quit. Would consider changing careers if I couldn't find a better situation.

Initially, this reaction has a potential for stagnation, but the later reactions are positive coping in nature. The danger here is that the individual could become trapped in the situation by age and benefit considerations, e.g., pensions, and run out of time to make positive changes.

Would take technical and management courses to keep myself stimulated.

Positive coping reaction if the courses truly represent new skills which will be used on the job. A borderline stagnation response if the courses have no practical or personal growth significance to the individual.

Can't accept your assumption. The organization is too dynamic and will have to change. I just can't believe that a situation like that would occur.

This, more than likely, is a stagnation response in that the individual is denying the problem and any need for concern or action on his part.

This analysis reveals several interesting points. First, there are two very clear-cut positive coping reactions: quitting and seeking fulfillment off the job. In these instances the individual is actively seeking an environment more suited to his needs. However, the on-the-job services of such individuals are either lost or reduced to their *current* organization. The individual gains, hopefully, but the organization loses, probably. Second, there are two stagnation or near-stagnation reactions: becoming indifferent and denying the problem. In these cases, it appears that the individual will stay with the organization—and stagnate. Then there are the mixed responses: try it, and if it doesn't work, quit and maybe change careers, take courses to stay stimulated, and empire building.

What does not emerge from this analysis is a positive coping response that would clearly benefit the individual as well as the organization. In other words, the middle managers do not see a clear-cut way in which they can continue to develop within the confines of their own organization. At best, to continue to develop they must change jobs, seek outside interests, or change careers. This really sums up the problems that middle managers face in coping with their work environment. They do not see their organization affording them viable avenues for continued growth or for significant change. Again, this is the boxing-in of which they complain. If they leave, they assume considerable risk and uncertainty as to whether the change ultimately will be of benefit to them. If they stay, they face stagnation at the other extreme, or some uncertainty as to whether they can achieve some degree of growth or change through the various mixed strategies they describe. Obviously, we need more positive coping options within organizations; these will be discussed in later chapters.

COPING WITH THE CRISIS

Now that we have looked at the reactions of the middle managers to the midlife crisis, let us consider in more detail some of the specific behaviors involved in these reactions.

JOB CHANGES

For some people job changes are a deliberate strategy for advancement to top executive positions. There is ample evidence to indicate that such moves, particularly between organizations, are associated with getting to the top jobs.[4] In other words, increasingly top corporate officers are individuals who have spent most of their careers in organizations other than the one they are now heading.

But what of the individuals who never make it to the top and are destined to spend their careers in the middle management rank? What are their mobility patterns like?

Professor John F. Veiga of the University of Connecticut has provided us with some excellent data on this subject.[5] From his research, which

[4]Eugene E. Jennings, *Routes to the Executive Suite.* New York: McGraw-Hill, 1971.

[5]John F. Veiga, "The Mobile Manager at Mid-Career," *Harvard Business Review* (January-February 1973).

involved 1,243 middle managers from three large manufacturing companies in Ohio, he identified several *distinct* sets of reasons for middle manager mobility as well as ascertaining the different ages at which mobility is apt to occur for each set of reasons:

Organization-initiated mobility. At about age 37 the manager who has proven himself in relatively small managerial assignments, and who is now regarded as seasoned, is moved to positions of broader responsibility in the middle management ranks. Such moves, which are initiated by the organization, can continue up to about age 55 and reflect, primarily, the needs and interests of the organization. During these years, if the individual is successful, he will break out of the middle management ranks into top management. If not, then he typically will spend the rest of his career in middle management.

Individual-initiated mobility. The individual also may initiate job changes, usually for both family and personal needs. Between the ages of 42 and 54 the person may initiate moves because he feels free of family-induced constraints. During this age period, the children are apt to have grown and left home and the middle manager no longer feels the pressures to stay in one place for the sake of continuity in his children's schooling, and so on. Between the ages of 42 and 48, Veiga found that job changes were based on personal needs, for example, to avoid being boxed in.

If we overlay the ages of these types of mobility, we find that approximately between the ages of 40 and 50 there are powerful forces which cause middle managers to change jobs. It would appear that the needs of the organization and the individual for job changes coincide in time, so as to permit meaningful job changes, that is, changes that are of benefit to the organization and the manager. This is an important point to keep in mind in terms of manpower planning as it affects middle managers. If the needs of the organization and the needs of the middle managers for mobility are looked at together, we may find that there is more opportunity to move middle managers than heretofore realized. This could be a positive step in relieving the boxing-in phenomenon.

CAREER CHANGES

Career change is really an extension of job change. In a job change basically the individual is seeking a more favorable environment; in career change the individual is seeking a new set of skills and a new environment in which to apply them. Sometimes a career change may involve the use of old skills in a radically new environment, for example, from manager of a manufacturing division to an executive director of a social service agency.

Just prior to the 1970–1971 recession, we began to see reports in the media about second careers. These typically involved people who were making a radical change in their working lives. Thus we read of an executive who became a director of a birth control agency, a Jewish lawyer who became a Protestant minister, and so forth. If it were not for the recession, second-career phenomenon may have become a more defined trend. It is obvious that a change in careers requires a favorable economic climate and/or some individual economic resources to support the transition. In many, but not all, instances the transition between careers requires some additional formal education.

Via education. Hiestand has provided us with the most systematic data about individuals who are attempting to change their careers after age 35 via the educational route. His study,[6] which is based on a sampling of 70 graduate students at Columbia University and who were over 35, is limited but, nonetheless, represents the best data available. The individuals pursuing full-time graduate study were doing so because they felt their skills were obsolete. They had developed new interests, new professions of interest to them had emerged since they originally graduated from college, or they had unsatisfied career aspirations, that is, they were entering a field that they could not enter earlier in their careers.

Hiestand also cites some data from other universities which give us an indication of the numbers of such people. For example, in 1966 16.5 percent of the professional and graduate students at New York University (full and part-time) were over 35. The comparable numbers at Columbia University and the University of Chicago during this same year were 20.4 and 8.7 percent, respectively. The full-time students over 35 years of age at New York University and Columbia University were 3.7 percent and 5.4 percent, respectively. These figures do not include graduate students, full or part-time, in the teaching professions, as this category normally attracts a large number of graduate students.

Hiestand feels that the number of individuals over 35 who will be part-time students will tend to increase although he offers no estimates of the rate of increase. His reasons to support this notion are the growing acceptability in our society for people in their middle years to make the change, a greater need on the part of individuals in this age bracket to make a change, and a general trend of favorable economic circumstances both on an individual and a larger society basis to support the educational efforts.

[6]D. L. Hiestand, *Changing Careers After 35.* New York: Columbia University Press, 1971.

At this point, we can only guess at the number of middle managers who are contemplating a career change via an educational effort or the number who might actually benefit from a move of this type. What we do know is that it is possible to make such a move.

Via avocation. Not all career changes involve additional education. In a surprising number of instances I have found that the individual's second career evolved from an avocational interest or a relatively small outside business interest that the person had developed and nurtured over a period of years.

In one case an engineering manager in an electronics firm had for a number of years developed a small-scale real estate and property management business to which he transitioned full-time in 1971. He gave as his reasons for developing this sideline his curiosity, a feeling that someday he might need a hedge against the uncertainties of the defense electronics business, and the fact that his job was not so demanding that it did not leave enough energy to pursue another interest.

In late 1970 he was laid off with literally no prospect for employment elsewhere in the area. He used his severance pay, unemployment insurance, and contributions to a pension program to support him while he transitioned his part-time business into a full-time one. These sources of financial support, in his estimate, were critical in making the transition. He also indicated that the recession accelerated his move, but that he ultimately would have done it anyhow as all he saw for himself in his company were "25 years of stagnation until retirement."

In another situation with which I am familiar, a middle manager made the transition to an initially small but now growing business through an avocation. In this case it involved the repair of cameras which he did as a hobby and in some respects as a challenge to his abilities and interests. The scarcity and special nature of his skills resulted in many demands for his services. He then formed his own business and is applying his managerial skills to this effort. He left his employer voluntarily.

Both situations illustrate something interesting about employment in our society. In 1972, for example, only 5.5 million people out of 80.2 million in the workforce were self-employed. Over 90 percent of those employed were on someone else's payroll. This really reflects a severe shortage of individuals who have the motivation, managerial skills, and access to financial resources to operate their own businesses. In many respects, small business efforts represent a good opportunity for many middle managers who feel thwarted in a large organization. A small business offers many opportunities to play all the business roles as well for financial gain. Many middle managers probably do not realize what they have to offer in small business situations. They may be worth looking at.

REDIRECTION OF EFFORT

For many people a job or career change is not possible, either psychologically or economically. They may feel that they have to give up too much to make a change or that they don't have enough to offer another company or in another career field. An individual who must keep his job and who is highly motivated to seek fulfillment but is not finding it on his job has the option of finding satisfaction off the job. There are no precise statistics on the number of people who cope with meaningless work in this way, but I have a distinct impression from my consulting work in industry and government that many middle managers are choosing this route.

In effect, this approach solves two problems for the manager. He keeps his job and the accompanying benefits and uses outside activities to help him develop and grow as an individual and to find more meaning in his life. In effect, the job supports his outside development activities. Typical outside activities which individuals cite as being meaningful are recreation, hobbies, community work, and seeking local political offices. This kind of coping is a good adjustment for the individual in that he can maintain his basic security needs while participating in some meaningful and fulfilling activities. For the organization, however, this adjustment usually means that the individual's best efforts probably are being applied elsewhere. Thus it represents a significant and hidden loss to the organization, although it is one which we are unable to measure at this time.

EDUCATION

Some middle managers try to keep stimulated through educational programs. There may be some useful, but limited, value in doing this through educational programs which deal with specific technical or managerial skills or with specific areas of knowledge. Attendance at some courses is mostly for mind-stretching. The manager is exposed to new ideas and has a stimulating intellectual experience.

Beyond these types of experiences, the value of the education approach does not appear to be significant. Many of the courses designed to stimulate his growth at times only serve to remind him of his limitations to take action in the organization based on this new knowledge. For example, I have been with middle managers in sessions on the subject of job enrichment. They very quickly grasp the concepts and methods and generally are in agreement with the approach and its intent.

Then we get to their role in implementing job enrichment in their organizations. At this point they start to cite the reasons why they could not do it in their organization. Some of these reactions may be regarded as defensive, but in some respects they are right. What they are saying is that the changes implied in the course far exceed their authority. The sessions usually end on a note of frustration, and frequently the parting comment is, "You should really have my boss in this course. He's the person who can make these changes." The managers leave with the feeling that their problems are not understood.

Another bad aspect of training programs is fragmentation of content; that is, the subject matter is not interrelated in a meaningful way in training programs. In particular, it is interrelated in a way that reflects what is happening in the organization and in a way that helps members of the organization to be more effective. For example, in conference room A a course on a new management information system is being held, while in conference room B there is a course on organizational relationships. A more effective course method is one course where the principles and problems of organizational relationships are explored in the context of a real-time management system, as the two affect each other in significant ways.

There is still one additional factor which lessens the value of development programs for middle managers. This is the fact that most such efforts are programmed. That is, they usually are designed with little regard for the needs of the individual manager. Even if there were a good procedure to do a development needs analysis, there is still the problem of resources in the organization, course material, time, and counselors to carry out individual programs for a large number of people.

Dr. Harry Levenson presents an excellent case for the role of the top executives—the managers of the middle managers—as teachers. He may be asking a lot from top executives, but he suggests they consider the following questions in considering their role as teachers:

> ...he [the executive] can ask these questions as a basing for his [teaching] efforts: What does the subordinate want to learn in the next year? How will that propel him toward more distant goals? How much of that can he learn in this position? What does he need to know of which he may as yet be unaware? What does the executive or the organization require him to know and how much of it is to be learned in the present experience? Combining the answers to these questions into a general statement, how can that generalization be subdivided into monthly, even weekly, units of experience and teaching?[7]

[7]Harry Levenson, *The Exceptional Executive*. Cambridge, Mass.: Harvard University Press, 1968.

Any executive or manager, at any level in the organization, who can acquire the skills to meet the intent of these questions can render an extremely valuable service to the people in his organization.

EMPIRE BUILDING AND EMPIRE MAINTENANCE

Empire building is frequently seen among middle managers. Some regard it as a form of job enrichment, particularly if he absorbs functions which are new to him. In this case he gets a double benefit: more authority and power as well as new functions to learn.

In order to build an empire a manager has to learn how to compete effectively for resources. The problem is that resources in an organization are relatively fixed, and the manager who learns to compete effectively usually wins at the expense of someone else—his fellow middle managers.

Edgar Schein[8] has described very aptly the effects of this type of win-lose competition in organizations. It typically results in the development of a high level of distrust between different parts of the organization and very poor communications between different segments. Over long periods of time this competitive environment literally can result in the development of stereotypes that different parts of the business have about each other: we're the good guys and you're the bad guys. Most interactions between the organization primarily then become attempts to support these stereotypes. Thus the real needs and the real issues of the organization are never adequately dealt with.

Keep in mind that these types of interpersonal relationships and communications are developing in that part of the organization which has the responsibility for planning, integrating, and controlling the management system. Thus we can see that the power-seeking tactics of some middle managers, while of value to them, can have strong negative effects in the organization.

Another aspect of empire building is empire maintenance. The motivation, of course, is to preserve one's status and authority, at least as measured by the size of one's organization. Here again, we find middle managers who have become experts at empire maintenance. Among their tactics are talking down the value of other departments, overtly and covertly; a short-run increase in effort and output to demonstrate effectiveness and worth to the organization; unwillingness to give up individuals for promotion (they may not be replaced); and a tendency to overvalue and overstate the performance of and need for individuals in the group. Of course, these tactics also contribute to the distrust and poor communications between organization components.

[8]E. H. Schein, *Process Consultation: Its Role in Organizational Development.* Reading, Mass.: Addison-Wesley, 1969.

ALCOHOLISM

There are no statistics on alcoholism which are specific to middle managers, but we can make some conservative estimates about the extent of the problem from fairly reliable national workforce data. My estimates are based on data from the National Council on Alcoholism.[9] The NCA estimate of national prevalence of alcoholism in 1968 shows a frequency (minimum) of 5.3 percent on the national level. Alcoholism in the workforce is constant at 5.3 percent for *all* segments of the workforce, meaning that alcoholism among middle managers is the same as that among blue collar workers. We can use the national level to estimate the number of visible alcoholics in the middle manager population. For the ease of arithmetic, and since we will be estimating anyhow, I will use 5 percent as the incidence figure. My deductions are:

- There are approximately 4 million middle managers in the United States as of March 1972.
- If we assume a 5 percent incidence rate, there are approximately 200,000 visible alcoholics in the middle manager ranks at this time.
- These are alcoholics who are at the later stages of the disease where the effects on their behavior and work performance are more visible. The 200,000 figure does not include middle managers whose drinking problem is so severe that they are unemployable, middle managers who are working in marginal occupations because of their drinking problem, or middle managers who have gone to skid row environments.
- Again, based on NCA estimates, we should assume that 10 percent of the 200,000 are under active treatment and will be cured. This nets out to approximately 180,000 visible alcoholics in the middle manager ranks today.

Do work-related factors cause drinking problems? The answer to this question is that we do not have an answer. The causes of alcoholism are extremely complex and not completely understood, and it is important that we imply no cause-and-effect relationships between work experiences and alcoholism. The safest approach is to treat it as a symptom.

There is only one study, by Trice and Belasco,[10] that deals adequately with the issue of whether work-related factors cause drinking. They

[9]*Labor Management Services Bulletin,* National Council on Alcoholism, March 18, 1971.

[10]H. M. Trice and J. A. Belasco, "The Aging Collegian: Drinking Pathologies Among Executive and Professional Alumni." In G. L. Maddox, ed., *The Domesticated Drug—Drinking Among Collegians.* New Haven, Conn.: College and University Press, 1970.

compared patterns of drinking behavior in college with subsequent patterns of drinking behavior after one had entered the workforce. Their data consisted of 552 questionnaire responses from members of Alcoholics Anonymous from all regions of the United States, plus 83 taped interviews from the New York City and Syracuse, New York, areas. The respondents described, in addition to such work behavior as absenteeism and work performance, their drinking histories when various problems related to alcohol began, the nature of these complications, and how early in their drinking history these complications began. One-quarter of the individuals who completed the questionnaires or who were interviewed were in professional or managerial positions.

In general, drinking problems which ultimately were regarded as alcoholism were not evident as part of the drinking pattern in college. The patterns that ultimately developed into alcoholism only became evident after a certain point in the individual's career. Typically it was when the person started to develop a specific commitment to his future, that is, a commitment to a specific organization after having changed jobs several times and to a very specific role or career path within this organization. Evidently, in college and early in one's career the individual felt he had flexibility and choice and social drinking was not a problem. In effect, the specific career choice as well as the elimination of alternatives and the consequences of success or failure in the specific field he had chosen triggered the drinking problem. The research data do not offer much evidence as to why the choice of a specific career path triggers alcoholism and how it relates to middle managers. If anything, the research points out how little we know in this area and the need for more analysis.

How to deal with an alcoholic employee is a sensitive subject but one which is getting more attention. Many companies now have programs which are geared toward handling alcoholism in the blue collar ranks. The basic strategy of these programs is to train foremen and supervisors to recognize the symptoms of alcoholism as they appear in the employee's job performance. Patterned absenteeism and tardiness and disappearance from the assigned work station are typical indicators of a probable drinking problem. The individual is confronted with his job performance and told that he stands to lose his job if he does not improve. Unions typically cooperate in this effort. The individual is given an opportunity to get help for his "problem" and if he continues to seek help, his job will not be jeopardized. In effect, the threat of losing one's job is used to get the individual to enter a program for alcoholics. There is no way of knowing if this approach is used in the middle manager ranks, but it would appear to be useful. There are undoubtedly enough alcoholic situations in the middle management ranks to warrant some attention to this problem.

DIVORCE

Divorce is included because it appears to be another outcome of the midcareer crisis: one may decide to change wives as well as careers. In the case of divorce data, it is not possible to make any estimates about the middle manager population as in the case of alcoholism. It is my impression, and I have confirmed this with several attorneys who specialize in divorce cases, that the divorce rate of persons at about age 40 is rising at a very rapid rate. The divorce pattern has the following characteristics:

- This age coincides with the peak of the midcareer crisis.
- This is the age at which the children have left home or are close to leaving home so that feelings about staying married for the sake of the children are no longer good rationalizations.
- Divorce is more acceptable today as a solution to marital problems.
- The economic consequences of divorce, while still significant, can be borne by the relatively more affluent middle managers.
- Divorce laws make divorce easier.

The only piece of data which even remotely supports the notion of a greater frequency of divorce at older ages is the increase in the median years of marriage at the time that the divorce takes place. This number is increasing, suggesting that more people are getting divorced after having been married for longer periods of time (and therefore are older). For example, in 1950 the median length of marriage at the time of divorce was 5.3 years while in 1968 (the latest year for which data are available) the median length of marriage at the time of divorce was 7.0 years.[11] Again, we should assume no cause-and-effect relationship between work-related factors and divorce as in the case of alcoholism.

What are the effects of divorce on the middle manager in terms of his career and performance? Thomas J. Murray, in *Dun's Review*, gives the results of a poll among two dozen major corporations about how they deal with divorce.[12] Generally it is regarded as a private affair and a hands-off attitude is maintained.

However, the article does suggest that the manager's performance deteriorates significantly during the divorce process. He is apt to be

---

[11]*Statistical Abstracts of the United States: 1971*, U.S. Bureau of the Census.
[12]Thomas J. Murray, "The High Cost of Executive Divorce," *Dun's Review* (October 1971).

preoccupied and to make poor decisions as a result. In some instances "executives" often equate failure in marriage with failure in their work and, consequently, their uncertainty begins to undermine the decisions they must make.

If the divorce rate continues to increase and if it does have the effects on performance that were described, then business organizations may have no choice but to develop ways to deal with these situations. Professor Lawrence Zeitlin of New York's Bernard Baruch College suggests that management might be better off giving an executive a leave of absence while he is getting a divorce.[13] This would be more beneficial, in the long run, than having the manager in the work situation where he may make inferior decisons. It is clear that the midcareer crisis is a syndrome, the effects of which are clearly seen in the work situation.

THE COSTS OF COPING

I was asked to write a "thought piece" by the Department of Health, Education and Welfare on middle managers for inclusion in *Work in America* (MIT Press, 1972). I was asked to give particular emphasis to the costs of middle manager coping and cost-benefit ratios associated with such attempts. I am not a financial analyst, but I think it would be of interest to look at some of the cost factors associated with coping.

CAREER CHANGES

Basically, there are two figures we would want to estimate in the area of career changes. First, how many people would be involved, and, second, what would be the cost of a career change and what benefit would accrue from it. We cannot assume that every individual will want a career change or will benefit from one. Our best guideline to those who actively are seeking career changes or a significant upgrading in their skills to pursue their present careers comes from Hiestand's data about people over 35 who are pursuing additional education. If we assume that approximately 6 million people are enrolled in colleges in the United States today and that approximately 10 percent of them are over 35 (using a round median of Hiestand's enrollment data), then we are talking about 600,000 individuals. We are talking about less than 1 percent of the total workforce who are actively involved in an educational upgrading endeavor of the type described by Hiestand. Let us assume that it was made easier for individuals to do this and that this would result in a

---

[13]Lawrence Zeitlin, in Thomas J. Murray, op. cit.

tripling of the number of people who would have such interests. We therefore would be talking about 1.8 million individuals who might use education or reeducation as a means of changing their careers or significantly upgrading their skills for their present jobs. This would represent a little more than 2 percent of the total workforce, and of course not all of these individuals would be middle managers. Those numbers relevant to how many would be interested in or take advantage of the education have to be regarded as purely speculative. They do not include people in company-sponsored programs or other such graduate school programs that typically attract people from industry.

Now, what would it cost to reeducate a person for a second career? Here I think we can make some estimates with a bit more confidence. If we assume that the average middle manager is making $20,000 a year (no addition for benefits) and that two years is necessary for such a reeducation program, we then need to think about a salary replacement cost of approximately $40,000. In other words, $40,000 to support this individual, assuming he would be supported at the same level as he was in his job, would have to come from somewhere. And let's also assume that two years of tuition under the program at $2,500 a year would come to $5,000. Then we would be talking about a total reeducation cost, including salary and tuition, of $45,000 per manager.

Now let's take a look at what we get back in return for this $45,000. Assume that we are dealing with an obsolescent manager (one who is contributing 50 percent of his capacity). Every year in which he works, we "overpay" him $10,000, which is a net loss. If we reeducate him at a cost of $45,000, and the reeducation brings him up to 100 percent effectiveness, in effect we would stop the loss of $10,000 per year of overpayment. If we look at the $10,000 as what we gain as a result of the reeducation, then we recoup the $45,000 investment in a little less than five years. For every year after this, we gain, by not incurring the loss.

Who would pay for the reeducation? There are different arguments that can be advanced for payment for the reeducation by at least three parties—the company, the individual himself, and the government. We might argue that the company exposed the individual to a management system which made him obsolete, and therefore they should incur a significant portion of the costs for his reeducation. In effect, this would be a tax on a company for misuse of an important resource. We could also argue that the individual allowed himself to be exposed to such a system without taking steps on his own to prevent his obsolescence, and therefore he also should be required to pay part of the costs for his reeducation. Finally, we might argue that the individual represents a valuable national resource, and that if he is to continue as such then the government should have some interest in providing for his reeducation.

ALCOHOLISM

The costs of alcoholism can be computed more directly and with more confidence. According to the National Council on Alcoholism a conservative approach to computing the costs of alcoholism is to assume that it represents 25 percent of the individual's salary. At an annual salary of $20,000, this would represent an annual hidden loss of $5,000 plus the effects on other people in the organization.

The costs of curing alcoholism do not appear to be significantly high. Some companies have internal programs primarily geared toward identifying the alcoholic and motivating him to seek help. The help usually is provided by an outside organization such as Alcoholics Anonymous and does not result in any direct cost to the employing organization. The only costs that would seem to be incurred are those involved in training managers and supervisors to deal with the alcoholic employee. My guess is that the costs for training and so on would be not more than the losses incurred by three or four alcoholic employees. The cost-benefit ratios in alcoholism are extremely high because of the low direct costs incurred by the organization.

HIDDEN COSTS

We have taken some examples for which reasonable estimates of costs can be made. However, the most significant costs of managerial coping are hidden. They do not show up directly as lost units of production. What price do you put on a poor decision, an ill-timed decision, lack of innovation and creativity, and lack of effort by a middle manager? What multiplier do you put on this price as the actions of the middle manager touch upon and affect dozens of people elsewhere in an organization? These intangibles are where the time and costs are—and they probably are very high.

chapter four

How Middle Managers Cope as a Group

IN EARLY 1973 I observed the counting of the ballots in a union representation election in a public transit authority in the northeast. A representative of the state labor commission, a representative from management, and the attorney for the petitioning union were the focal point of attention. The ballots were counted and the number verified, and the challenged ballots were set aside. The state labor commission representative then started the count. It was a fairly monotonous cadence of yes... yes... yes, interrupted by an occasional no. It very quickly became apparent that the petitioners would win, and they did. There was a smattering of applause and handshakes around, and the winners went off to celebrate a four-year legal and legislative effort to establish their union.

MANAGER UNIONS

These proceedings are not unusual as union representation elections happen everyday. What made this situation different was that the ballots being counted were cast *by the middle managers* of this organization. They now have a union, and the management will bargain with them. Either this union representation election may be just an isolated incident, or in future years we may look back and see it as just the beginning of many such events. Which way it will go, of course, will depend on our organizations and legislatures.

Let's consider the events that led this group of middle managers (approximately 200) to form a union. We cannot and should not attempt to generalize from this situation, but we can get some helpful insights. The sequence of events in this situation is approximately as follows:

- In the late 1960s the union-represented employees of this organization achieved very significant wage gains. The gains were such that they overlapped or severely compressed the salary structure of the middle managers.
- Top management, in response to complaints from the middle managers, agreed to adjust their salaries in order to achieve greater equity.
- Top management then rated each of the middle managers on a ten-point scale and the salary increases were in direct proportion to the ratings. There was a factor of 10 between the smallest and largest increases granted. This was the first time this procedure had been used.
- The middle managers were quite upset by this process as in their eyes it did not reestablish their salary positions relative to the hourly union-represented wage structure.
- At this point, the middle managers started union organization efforts in which they had to overcome several legal obstacles before they finally won.

It is obvious that top management had the right intentions here—to relieve the inequities created by the large increases in the hourly union-represented group. The problem is that they used a pay for performance rating approach when an across-the-board adjustment might have been more appropriate. The across-the-board adjustment, depending on its size, would have relieved the compression and inequity for each middle manager to the same degree. In other words, it would have restored him to the same relative position he had vis-à-vis the hourly union-represented employee. The pay for performance merit-based increases restored some individuals, but not others, and also served to increase the salary differentials among the middle managers at a time when salary was an emotional issue for the *entire* group.

All of this is history, of course, and with our usual brilliant hindsight we can offer top management lots of advice on what they might have done differently. More importantly, however, we should look to the future, and consider what can cause this bit of management history to repeat itself.

In September 1971, the American Management Associations conducted a survey[1] of 526 middle managers and 572 personnel executives to assess the attitudes of these groups toward manager unions and the

[1]Alfred T. DeMaria, Dale Tarnowieski, and Richard Gurman, *Manager Unions?* AMA Research Report, 1972.

underlying reasons for any pro-union sentiment. Keep in mind several things regarding this survey. First, it was conducted at about the end of the 1970–1971 recession, when the recession and its effects were fresh in people's minds. Second, the persons who responded represented about 15 to 20 percent of the persons who received questionnaires. We don't know what those who didn't respond had to say about this issue. There is the possibility that the persons who responded had the strongest feelings about the issue. In other words, we're not certain about how representative this sample is of middle managers. All in all, they are the best data we have, and with these reservations in mind, we shall attempt to interpret what they mean.

Table 2 shows the receptiveness of the persons surveyed to collective bargaining, changes in the law which would permit it for managers, and informal groups to discuss various issues with top management. As can be seen, there is strong agreement among personnel executives (who presumably are in close touch with the middle manager situation in their

Table 2. Receptiveness of survey respondents to the key statements listed below.

According to Personnel Executives		Key Statements	According to Middle Managers	
Agree	Disagree		Agree	Disagree
335 (59%)	235 (41%)	Middle management is somewhat more receptive to the idea of collective bargaining today than it was, say, before the current economic recession.	340 (65%)	187 (35%)
160 (28%)	408 (72%)	Present laws should be changed to permit supervisory and middle management personnel to organize for the purpose of collective bargaining, if they so desire.	240 (47%)	272 (53%)
352 (62%)	214 (38%)	Middle managers should be allowed to organize informal groups to discuss conditions of employment with top management on a company-by-company basis.	387 (75%)	132 (25%)

SOURCE: Alfred T. DeMaria, Dale Tarnowieski, and Richard Gurman, *Manager Unions?* AMA Research Report, 1972.

organization), managers who would join unions, and managers who would not join unions that middle management is more receptive to the idea of collective bargaining now (September 1971) than it was before the recession.

Table 3 indicates that the managers who would join unions felt very strongly (95 percent) that the present laws should be changed to permit managers to organize if they so desire. In fact, supervisory and managerial employees have the right to form or join a union (Sec. 14(a) of the National Labor Relations Act). However, there is no legal requirement for the employer to bargain with, or even recognize, a union organization composed entirely of supervisory personnel. Thus, in effect, union membership has no teeth, as recognizing and bargaining with a middle manager union would be a voluntary act by the organization. Somewhat surprisingly, 28 percent of the personnel executives and 36 percent of the managers who would not join a union also favored changes in the law. Again,

Table 3. Managerial receptiveness to collective bargaining.

According to Managers Who Would *Join a Managers' Union*		Statement	According to Managers Who *Would* Not *Join a Managers' Union*	
Agree	Disagree		Agree	Disagree
92 (95%)	4 (5%)	Middle management is somewhat more receptive to the idea of collective bargaining today than it was, say, before the current economic recession.	248 (57%)	183 (43%)
92 (95%)	4 (5%)	Present laws should be changed to permit supervisory and middle management personnel to organize for the purpose of collective bargaining, if they so desire.	148 (36%)	268 (64%)
91 (94%)	6 (6%)	Middle managers should be allowed to organize informal groups to discuss conditions of employment with top management on a company-by-company basis.	296 (70%)	126 (30%)

SOURCE: Alfred T. DeMaria, Dale Tarnowieski, and Richard Gurman, *Manager Unions?* AMA Research Report, 1972.

all three groups felt that informal groups of middle managers should be organized to discuss issues with top management.

We would have to interpret the data as indicating that there has been a marked shift in sentiment in the middle management ranks to some form of collective action, with a marked preference for informal groups. There has been much visible and publicized evidence in our society as to what well-organized special interest groups (unions, blacks, Chicanos, women) can achieve, and perhaps the realization is growing in middle managers that they have to do something collectively in order to improve their situation. The middle managers do not seem ready, as yet, to take very formal action backed by legal support.

Figure 2 shows the percentages of managers, by age, who would join a managers' union if one were organized in their company. There are several ways of looking at these data. One is to take comfort in the fact that 65 percent would not join and hope we could get the 17 percent who are uncertain to share these feelings. A second way is to wonder about what portion of the 17 percent who were uncertain could be convinced to join the 18 percent who said yes. I asked several union business agents whether it would be worth their while to go after a group where, in the advance of any campaign, 18 percent of the members definitely would join, 17 percent were uncertain, and 65 percent said they would not join. The answers were emphatic yeses. Disregarding the problems of legal recognition for the moment, the business agents saw this situation as tempting.

A third way to look at the data is to look at the age groupings. Among the youngest middle managers (age 20 to 29), we find the greatest pro-union sentiment; of course, this is the group that is destined to be in middle management for many years to come. This group could very well be the forerunner of support for future manager unions.

In the AMA survey the managers were asked to select three items from a prepared list of 19 which in their opinion were most likely to produce middle management discontent and alienation from top management. The results are shown in Table 4. As can be seen, compensation (items 1 and 2 combined) emerges as number one, followed by lack of involvement in decision making and insufficient authority (items 4 and 5 combined) and growing concern about job security (item 3). These issues would seem to be the major ones. Compensation and job security could be reflective of inflation and the large wage gains in the blue collar ranks relative to those of the middle managers. Lack of involvement in decision making and insufficient authority probably are of longer standing and conceivably could have been first were it not for the current compensation and job security issues. The write-in essay responses, according to the AMA researchers, support this contention.

Let us now turn to an assessment of the potential for manager unions.

PLUS FACTORS

Issues exist. At the moment, pay inequities and job security most likely would trigger management unions. These issues are measurable and are

2. Percentage of middle managers by age group who would join a manager's union if one were organized in their companies.

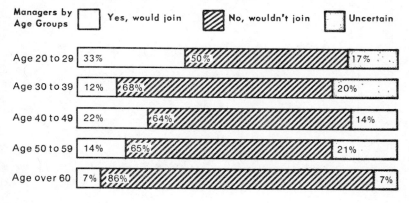

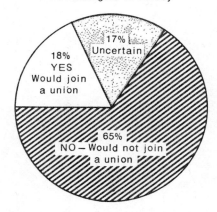

All Managers in Survey

SOURCE: Alfred T. DeMaria, Dale Tarnowieski, and Richard Gurman, **Manager Unions?** AMA Research Report, 1972.

Table 4. Conditions likely to increase middle management frustration and discontent with and alienation from top management according to responding middle managers by age group.

Conditions	Number of Middle Managers				
	Age 20–29	*Age 30–39*	*Age 40–49*	*Age 50–59*	*Age Over 60*
Gains of blue collar unions outpacing gains of management employees	20	68	85	37	5
Low salaries or salary inequities	14	69	64	40	5
Growing uncertainty about job security	10	46	68	32	4
Feeling of not being involved in decision-making process	11	37	48	27	5
Increased responsibility without increased authority	4	44	42	33	2
Little feeling of personal reward and achievement	6	43	41	17	4
Long hours without extra compensation	10	32	33	17	2
Lack of top management responsiveness to new ideas, improved methods	13	30	36	12	—

Decreased advancement opportunities	7	28	37	12	2
Impression that top management is locked away in an ivory tower	3	17	33	11	5
Unsatisfactory benefit packages	6	19	29	9	3
Increasingly bureaucratic tendencies of some larger corporations	4	6	29	12	2
Little opportunity for independent thought or action in running department	3	18	18	13	—
Belief that top management doesn't pass down adequate information	2	10	19	12	1
Increasing difficulty in career planning	1	5	12	13	1
Family life too disrupted by way the company operates	5	11	10	2	—
Unsatisfactory grievance procedures	1	6	11	3	—
Limited opportunity to keep up with new developments	2	4	5	2	1
Substantial influx of women into top management positions	—	1	1	2	—

SOURCE: Alfred T. DeMaria, Dale Tarnowieski, and Richard Gurman, *Manager Unions?* AMA Research Report, 1972.

ones which cause considerable pain—both in pocketbook and to the ego. Also they are concerns which blue collar unions have dealt with quite successfully. Their wage gains in recent years have in effect caused the inequities in the middle management ranks. And, of course, job security based on seniority is the mainstay of union contracts. If these were the only issues managers wanted to solve, then a managers' union is an ideal, known, and proven vehicle for doing so.

Emergence of special-interest action groups. In the last decade we have seen numerous constituencies who have strongly pushed their special interests. These groups have confronted our institutions and persons in authority and have captured a good deal of time and space in the media. Moreover, they have succeeded in attaining some of their objectives. The message is clear. If a special-interest group wants to achieve certain objectives, then it has to organize and pursue these objectives in an aggressive fashion. The middle managers have not done this but the models for the action are there.

Top management insensitivity. Top management's mishandling of a management problem could become a plus for the formation of manager unions. An example of an actual event illustrates this point. As a group, middle managers in an old manufacturing organization with a strong blue collar union requested that top management make some adjustments in their benefits to maintain some traditional differentials with the blue collar workforce. Top management turned them down abruptly and with little explanation. The middle managers then formed an association and pressed harder for the proposed changes. Top management refused to deal with them through the association. The middle managers eventually set up a picket line to bring attention to their demands and to enlist the support of the blue collar workers. Of course, they had no legal right to picket, but they saw this as a desperation tactic. Top management responded by firing the leaders and giving the remaining middle managers one hour to get back to work—which they did.

Perhaps this is an extreme example of top management insensitivity, but it is indicative of how management might choose to react. The middle managers in this organization have not formed a union, but given the legal sanction they undoubtedly would.

MINUS FACTORS

Lack of militancy among middle managers. We have not heard much from the middle managers as a group. We know that there is a lot of discontent in their ranks, but they are grumbling rather than shouting.

And they certainly aren't making their problems known, in or out of their organizations, in a collective fashion. The problem here, of course, is that the audience for their complaints is the top management of their organizations, who also happen to be their bosses and who also happen to exert a lot of "fate control" over them.

In the AMA survey just about half the middle managers felt that top management would strongly oppose the idea of discussing conditions of employment on an informal basis with them and about the same number indicated that fear of reprisal would thwart attempts to organize informal groups. This may not be so, but this is what they believe.

Lack of legal protection. Stated very simply, middle managers (all supervisors, in fact) do not enjoy the same legal protection as do blue collar workers in regard to unions. They can organize, but the law does not require management to recognize them or to bargain with them. This lack of legal protection and the expressed fear of reprisal may account for the lack of militancy in this group.

Managers distrust union methods and unions don't have much interest in organizing managers. My surmise is that if middle managers are organized, the leadership will have to come from within their ranks. In other words, it will have to be someone with whom they can identify. The middle managers are distrustful of blue collar union leaders and methods, due largely to differences in education and status.

I have talked informally with about a half dozen blue collar union business agents about their perceptions of organizing middle managers, and I do not sense any great enthusiasm on their part either. They have trouble understanding why middle managers would even want to organize, and they are not sure how they would approach them. Obviously, they have thought of it before.

Middle managers see very few gains from unions. Managers are very conservative about what they expect to get from unions. Responding managers in the AMA survey who would join a union considered increased job security, salaries, and benefits as the major gains. Beyond this, the list drops off rapidly. I would argue that because of their strategic location in the organization, the middle managers could gain much more from being organized than they realize. The problem is that the middle managers have never organized and thus do not have much experience in the strategic use of the power of an organized group. Let's take the public utility industry as an example of how an organized middle management can exert considerable leverage.

From time to time, there have been strikes in the public utilities in the Boston area. One of the interesting things about these strikes is the uninterrupted service, and these are strikes that have endured for several months. It may take longer to get a phone installed or fixed, but generally the service is satisfactory. Executives in the utility industry will tell you that efficiency goes up during strikes. Why? Because the middle managers are manning the operations on 12-hour shifts. Generally, there is a high dedication to the public in utility organizations and this comes through in the efforts of the middle managers during strikes.

But what if they were organized and their union were not directly involved in the strike? Here are some things they could do:

1. They could cross the picket lines of the other unions and refuse to do the work of the union members who are on strike. This would have the effect of closing down the operations.
2. They could refuse to cross the picket lines which also would have the effect of closing down the operations.
3. They could cross the picket lines and agree to do the work of the members of other unions. This would keep the operations going.

The third option, of course, is the one with the greatest strategic potential. In effect, the continuance or discontinuance of the operations would be in the hands of the middle managers. It would seem to me that this option would considerably enhance their power vis-à-vis top management. (As an aside, we might consider the situation where the middle managers went out on strike and everyone else came to work. What would be the effect of their absence on the operations of the organization? I'm sure there are many middle managers who would rather not have this question answered.)

THE CONSENSUS

In balance, there seem to be stronger arguments against managers organizing than there are for. While the pay inequity and job security issues are visible and could serve as focal points for an organizing effort, the lack of legal protection, militancy, and an awareness of the potential power that a union would give them and fear of reprisals argue too strongly against manager unions. Middle managers who organized, at the present time, would not have much to gain in that top management would not be required to recognize or bargain with them. They might find ways of getting top management to do so voluntarily, but this is quite chancy. On the other hand, they could lose quite a bit—their jobs, for example. Clearly, the law would have to be changed to give managers the same rights as blue collar and nonsupervisory professionals before we can expect to see any organizing attempts in the middle management ranks.

Well, where does this leave us in terms of how middle managers cope with their situation on an individual or a group basis? The picture is not encouraging, from both the view of the managers and the organizations. There do not appear to be any coping mechanisms which satisfy both sets of interests. The positive coping reactions—those in which the middle manager generates some positive and hopefully satisfying change—occur outside the organization. These reactions typically involve job and career changes and redirection of effort for which limited opportunities may exist in the organization. The individuals who go the positive coping route are the ones who typically maintain the vitality and zest to keep developing at later stages in their lives. These individuals would then represent a loss to the organization. The stagnation reactions, apathy and denial, involve a somewhat passive acceptance of the situation. These are the people who then begin to typify the graying of middle managers—passive, inflexible, and bureaucratic, who in time become a problem for themselves and the organization.

Group action by the middle managers which might force some positive change is not on the horizon. There are many real factors which argue against collective efforts, and the managers themselves see gains only in the hygiene areas, that is, pay, benefits, job security.

Something has to give somewhere or organizations will continue to lose (and fail to attract) those people for whom growth as a human being is an important objective, and they will continue to keep those who can accept and tolerate stagnation. In time, this will continue to produce an inept middle management structure.

chapter five

The Class of '67:
The Next Generation
of Middle Managers

IN THE 1960s a remarkable transition occurred on our university campuses. The Sputnik-induced education boom resulted in a marked growth in the college population, the number of colleges and universities, and faculty size. Of course, we also had the students to fill these universities. The postwar baby boom assured this.

In addition to growth in sheer numbers, there was also a remarkable change in the behavior of college students. No longer were they content with the typical campus capers. Rather, certain groups began to espouse "radical" views directed at basic changes in our society. This was really not new, as we have always had radical elements on campuses. What was new was the fact they they captured the attention of the media, and through sheer persistence and snowballing support on and off the campus, they brought about some major changes in our society. At a minimum, they jolted us from our paternalistic acceptance of their capers as a last fling before getting down to the serious business of life. Generally, we now have learned to regard them as a constituency capable of exerting considerable force in our society. We need only look at what they did in their college years, prior to the time they even could vote, as proof of this.

We have always had a tradition of focusing on campus life and events, and in the 1960s we did it to even a greater extent. With this fixed focus, we can learn quite a bit about successive generations of college students. But what happens when the student graduates from college, particularly in the five to six years immediately following graduation? It is at this stage, early career development, for which there are little data.

In this chapter we will attempt to fill this gap. As best we can, we will track the class of '67 through this early period in their careers, concentrating on a number of broad themes: (1) the significance of the events in their lives as they grew up, (2) their early career experiences, and (3) an analysis of how they might approach the role of middle managers.

THE NEXT GENERATION OF MIDDLE MANAGERS

Why the class of '67? We do not mean to imply that they are different from other graduating classes of the mid- to late 1960s. We chose them as being representative of these graduates and because the class of '67 happens to fit certain interesting criteria.

First, to use a term originated by Margaret Mead, they are "the oldest postwar people." If we assume that they were 22 years old when they graduated from college in 1967, then they were born in 1945, coinciding with the end of World War II. Their lives therefore have been shaped by the events which have occurred since World War II. Second, they now are approximately 28 years old. Those who entered industry upon graduation and have made normal progress in their organizations are on the threshold of becoming middle managers. Some probably already are middle managers. Third, they are on the front side of the midcareer crisis.

As a reference point, we will compare the class of '67 to the class of '51 (assuming that this group had no military service in World War II and in the Korean conflict until after their graduation from college). The class of '51 was born in 1929 and is now 45 years old. By now, they are well entrenched in middle manager positions and are on the far side of the midcareer crisis. They also are in the modal age group of middle managers.

The following chart shows the political, economic, social, and technological events that have occurred in the lifetimes of these two groups to date (1974). The class of '51 was born the year the Depression started, and their early and midteen age years were dominated by World War II. They were in college after the war and shared this experience with large numbers of older and more mature World War II veterans. They entered the workforce or fulfilled their military service right after the start of the Korean conflict. They entered the business world during the first postwar expansion of the 1950s during the relatively stable years of the Eisenhower administration.

The external circumstances of the class of '67 during their formative

A COMPARISON OF THE EVENTS IN THE LIVES OF THE CLASS OF '51 AND THE CLASS OF '67

Year	Class of '51 Age	Class of '67 Age	Events
1929	Born	A	Depression begins, stock market crashes
1930	1	N	
1931	2	C	
1932	3	I	World War I veterans march on Washington
1933	4	E	All banks in U.S. closed, prohibition ends, Hitler becomes chancellor of Germany
1934	5	N	
1935	6	T	Class of '51 enters first grade, Social Security Act passed
1936	7	H	Spanish Civil War starts
1937	8	I	
1938	9	S	Germany invades Austria
1939	10	T	World War II starts
1940	11	O	
1941	12	R	U.S. enters World War II
1942	13	Y	
1943	14		Class of '51 enters high school
1944	15		
1945	16	Born	End of World War II, FDR dies, first atomic bomb exploded
1946	17	1	War crime trials in Germany
1947	18	2	Class of '51 enters college
1948	19	3	Truman elected, Berlin blockade starts
1949	20	4	Russians explode atomic bomb

Year			
1950	21	5	Start of Korean conflict
1951	22	6	Class of '51 graduates from college, class of '67 enters first grade, transcontinental television inaugurated
1952	23	7	Eisenhower elected
1953	24	8	Korean cease-fire
1954	25	9	Supreme Court declares school desegregation unconstitutional
1955	26	10	Bus boycott in Alabama
1956	27	11	Eisenhower reelected
1957	28	12	Russians launch Sputnik
1958	29	13	First U.S. satellite orbited
1959	30	14	Class of '67 enters high school
1960	31	15	Kennedy elected president, lunch counter sit-ins start, 76,000 students participate in sit-ins
1961	32	16	Russians launch first human into space, first American launched into space
1962	33	17	First American orbits the earth
1963	34	18	200,000 people demonstrate for civil rights in Washington, class of '67 enters college, Kennedy assassinated
1964	35	19	Johnson elected
1965	36	20	Increased U.S. involvement in Vietnam
1966	37	21	Economy starts to boom, inflation starts, ghetto riots, Vietnam protests start
1967	38	22	Class of '67 graduates, ghetto riots
1968	39	23	Nixon elected
1969	40	24	First moon landing
1970	41	25	Recession
1971	42	26	Recession
1972	43	27	Recession ends, Nixon reelected
1973	44	28	End of U.S. involvement in Vietnam, Watergate affair
1974	45	29	Energy crisis

years were quite different from those of the class of '51. They entered the first grade the year transcontinental television was inaugurated. The Supreme Court decision banning school desegregation was issued when they were in the fourth grade. Sputnik and the first American satellite came in the seventh and eighth grades. During their high school years space exploration intensified, President Kennedy was elected, the lunch counter sit-ins occurred, and the first human beings were orbited into space. In September of 1963 they entered college and in November of the same year President Kennedy was assassinated. During their college years United States involvement in Vietnam escalated, civil rights demonstrations increased in frequency and intensity, university presidents were locked in or thrown out of their offices, pot became an issue, the rules of universities governing the behavior of students were relaxed considerably, the economy was booming, and the job market for the new college graduate was exceptionally good. In the spring of their graduation year President Johnson indicated that he would not seek reelection. This was pretty heady stuff. Youth was worshipped in the media and by the marketeers, and they had demonstrated their power to bring about change even before they could vote.

Thus we see quite a contrast in the backgrounds of the classes of '51 and '67. The class of '51 grew up in times of economic hardship and conflict with overseas foreign powers. Education was their ticket to a better economic future. The class of '67, on the other hand, grew up in a period of very concentrated changes—social, political, technological, and economic. They were prominent in the groups demanding social and political changes *within* our country. Thus their efforts were not directed at foreign enemies but at some basic social and political institutions within our own society.

Well, what happens to a group like this when they enter the world of work? The first thing that happens is that they are dispersed. (Many, of course, do not enter the world of work. They go on to professional graduate schools.) They may retain their long hair and beards (now also shared by many of their elders) but basically they are entering a new organization and power structure which is unfamiliar to them and against which they have yet to be tested.

We might get a better understanding of their situation as new entrants into the workforce if we track their careers in the initial years. Typically, they come into a business organization through a functional area and/or entrance training program. According to Schein[1] the early work years

[1]Edgar H. Schein, "How to Break In the College Graduate," *Harvard Business Review* (November-December 1964), pp. 68–76.

for the new graduate are a period of socialization, a period when they learn their roles and start to acquire the attitudes and values of the organization. In terms of role acquisition, Schein found that the early years can be quite critical to future advancement. The young graduates whose early assignments, for example, are challenging and demanding tend to advance at a faster rate in the early years than those who have unchallenging and undemanding assignments. The rationale for this is that the young graduate who is challenged very early develops a set of expectations about what is required of him—in this case a lot. His achievement level is recognized in terms of larger salary increases and other assignments with challenging responsibilities. As this process is repeated, he begins to outpace his peers and is recognized as someone with high potential. This in turn gets him on the fast track and, if his performance is sustained, he quickly finds himself in a position with supervisory and managerial responsibilities.

The tricky part of this process is that a great deal depends on chance, that is, on the early assignments one is given. To the achievement-oriented new college graduate, initial challenging assignments can be very satisfying and rewarding in terms of what the organization has to offer him. But what happens when the initial assignments are not challenging? The most likely result, particularly when jobs are plentiful, is turnover.

I have some unpublished data from a 1968 analysis I conducted of turnover among new college graduates. They were participants in a three-year prestigious management training program in a large company. By the end of the third year, nearly 60 percent of the trainees had resigned. Interviews with trainees six to twelve months after they had voluntarily left revealed that the low level of the training assignments (in their eyes) caused them to look elsewhere. Certain assignments, such as routine clerical auditing, produced almost 100 percent turnover.

When queried on the characteristics of desirable entrance or training assignments, the interviewees responded as follows:

They want work which is perceived as important to the organization. Many of the trainees felt that their assignments did not represent work which was important to the organization. For example, one trainee indicated that he was asked to audit a large number of expense accounts, most of which were six to twelve months old. His perception was that these expense states had been accumulated until a warm body became available to check them out. He happened to be it, and whether or not this work got done appeared to be of no great consequence to the organization.

They want work which presents an opportunity to learn. The trainees consider their assignments as opportunities to learn and are frustrated when few such learning situations occur. An examination of the "low learning" assignments very quickly revealed an interesting pattern. The manager who had the training assignment was using the trainee as "efficiently" as possible. From his point of view efficiency meant getting maximum output from the trainee with minimum effort on the part of the manager and other people in his organization. The training usually involved teaching the trainee something he could learn to do in one or two weeks and then having him do this work for the remainder of the assignment. The manager's reasoning, of course, is why invest a lot of time in training someone who will not be around very long. The result is that the trainee does not learn very much.

They want to be part of the decision-making process. Decision making was a very sensitive area to both the trainees and the managers. The trainees wanted to get to where the "management action" was. At a minimum, they wanted an opportunity to observe how decisions were made, for example, by sitting in on meetings where important matters were being decided. The trainees also felt that there were times when they could make a contribution to the decision-making process. Many managers reacted negatively. They saw the trainees as being unrealistic, with little of value to contribute. Groups of managers talked about the trainees as feeling they "would become vice presidents after six months on the job."

They wanted a clearer perception of the career paths. The trainees appeared to have a high tolerance for routine and low learning assignments if they knew to where the assignments led. After all, the training period was finite, and if something more desirable could be seen at the end of the training period, then they could wait it out. When they could not see something better, they left.

One interesting point in the follow-up on this analysis was the reaction of the managers. When they were confronted with the data and the suggestions for upgrading the assignments, they became very defensive. One of their more frequent reactions was to point out that an assignment which was rated very low by the trainees had been their initial assignment when they joined the company—a "if it was good enough for me it should be good enough for them" type of philosophy. Of course the managers failed to recognize the many changes in the 15 or so years since they entered the workforce, notably what people learn in college today versus 20 years ago and the higher level of expectation about what they will do and how they will be utilized.

Turnover among the new college graduate is not a particularly new phenomenon. There is always turnover "spike" in the first three to four years of employment. This usually is the period when the new graduate is zeroing in more specifically on his interests and aptitudes and the type of work that will satisfy him, and it may take several job changes before this learning takes place. For the class of '67, however, this turnover was intensified further by the competition for the new graduate as well as by the higher expectations they had regarding how their skills would be utilized in the work situation.

THE QUIET REVOLUTION

In terms of overt manifestations, the chronicle of the class of '67 seems to end coincident with the 1970–1971 recession. We have not heard very much from this group since then, and we certainly have not seen any actions by them in the business world comparable to their tactics on the campuses in the 1960s. Does this mean that the prophecy of many of their elders, that they would settle down and become "like us," has come true? Some settling down probably has taken place, as it is normal for people in their twenties to be concerned with finishing the psychological work of leaving home and of establishing themselves as adults in work, marriage, and so on; and there is no reason to believe that the class of '67 is forgoing these stages of development.

We should not assume, however, that these preoccupations preclude change in the work situation. The class of '67 is bringing about change, but the change is in the form of a "quiet revolution" as opposed to the noisy one in which they were involved on the campus.

The changes that are being brought about by the class of '67 are intertwined in their work and life-styles. It is not really possible to separate the two because they overlap and affect each other. Perhaps the biggest change we are seeing in younger management employees is that they are less willing to play top management's game in the way top management would like to see it played. I am referring here to the "career ladder" game, which, in many respects, is the only game in town and one which serves the interests of top management very well. The career ladder game calls for individuals to compete for material rewards through advancement. It generally assures that the better people will move up because the rewards for moving up are quite attractive (money, status, power). The typical paraphernalia of this game are training programs, assessment centers, career planning, compensation systems, rotational moves, development assignments, and so on. This is not a bad game if enough of the right people play it. For those who are interested and succeed in it, it can be very rewarding. But what if large numbers of the right people refuse to play the game? And this appears to be part of the quiet revolution of the class of '67. They are not interested in playing the career ladder game as top management intended it; rather they are using it to serve their own needs.

Perhaps the greatest evidence of this unwillingness to play the career ladder game is the increasing refusal on their part to accept promotions if it involves personal inconvenience. In other words they have added another dimension to the career ladder game, personal comfort and convenience. There is a growing unwillingness to sacrifice some degrees of personal comfort and convenience for the sake of material gain.

Beckhard[2] indicates that the increased refusal to accept promotions also is evident in managers in their forties who are putting personal criteria ahead of organizational criteria. They are discovering that they can be financially free of their organizations at relatively early ages. In other words, they don't have to work to age 65 to support their retirement; they don't strive to leave their children large estates; health insurance provides protection against financial disaster in old age; and their financial burdens are eased in their forties when the children start to leave home. The older managers have finally discovered something that the class of '67 has known and experienced throughout their lives: relative freedom from economic need.

A sound psychological rationale for this shift in behavior in younger and older managers is found in Maslow's hierarchy of needs and the principles relating to these needs.[3] The lower-order needs are primarily survival and security, which in our society quickly translate into a reasonably well-protected source of income. The higher-order needs deal with justice and achieving individuality and growth. A key principle in Maslow's theory is that once a need is satisfied it is no longer a motivator. When we apply this to the older and younger managers, we can see what is happening.

Because the older managers, in many instances, are becoming relatively free of economic constraints and are less motivated by company policies, they are becoming more concerned with the higher-order needs of individuality and growth. Refusal of promotions (material gains) over personal convenience, therefore, is a natural development. The younger managers, generally, have been free of economic concerns and they *start* their careers with psychological needs that have a stronger emphasis

[2]Richard Beckhard, "Mutiny in the Executive Ranks," *Innovation* (May 1972).
[3]Abraham H. Maslow, *Motivation and Personality,* 2nd edit. New York: Harper & Row, 1970.

on the higher-order needs. Not that they are not interested in material and economic matters, but their needs in the economic area are satisfied relatively early in their careers. They start out concerned with individuality and growth whereas the older managers took some years to get there. As long as we have a reasonably good economy we can expect these higher-order needs to predominate, and management styles and practices will have to be responsive to them.

This shift in emphasis from lower-order to higher-order needs does not appear to be a transient phenomenon. The College Placement Council periodically surveys a sample of approximately 100,000 members of incoming freshman classes in regard to their values. The most recent surveys indicate a high degree of emphasis on self and on growth in the incoming freshman classes of 1968 and 1970.[4,5]

Yankelovich,[6] who has conducted an in-depth study of the changes in student values, reports significant changes in attitudes toward authority, desired career rewards, and work. Only 36 percent of the students in his 1971 survey did not mind the prospect of being bossed on the job as compared to 56 percent in 1967. Approximately 80 percent of the students believe that a meaningful career is important. However, career choices are based on such factors as the opportunity to make a contribution, job challenge, the ability to find self-expression, and free time for outside interests. He indicates that job prestige continues to rank at the very bottom of factors cited.

Approximately 70 percent of the students no longer believe that hard work will pay off—not that they are unwilling to work hard but that hard work is no longer considered the "royal road to success." Yankelovich reports that a majority rank the importance of work well behind love, friendship, education, and self-expression. If work is to be meaningful to young people, then it must satisfy needs that are important to them, such as an opportunity to make a contribution and self-expression. Concomitantly, top management will have to deal with the new attitude toward authority.

The upward shift to higher-order needs is more pervasive than the rejection of material opportunities for personal need satisfaction. We actually may be witnessing a transition in the success ethic which will

---

[4]*Trends in Academic and Career Plans of College Freshmen, Report No. 1.* Bethlehem, Pa.: CPC Foundation, 1972.

[5]*Career Plans of College Graduates of 1965 and 1970, Report No. 2.* Bethlehem, Pa.: CPC Foundation, 1973.

[6]Daniel Yankelovich, *The Changing Values on Campus: Political and Personal Attitudes of Today's College Students.* New York: Washington Square Press, 1972.

have far-reaching implications for how we develop and manage managers. In his comprehensive and richly detailed book *The American Idea of Success,* Richard M. Huber charts the progression of the success ethics in our society.[7] According to Huber, ours has always been an egalitarian society, and it didn't really matter who your parents were. Although the status of your parents might in many ways influence your ultimate status, you did not inherit the status of your parents for life. Material success was the measure of progress and upward status.

The prevailing success ethics in our society, generally, have supported and rationalized material success. In colonial times, material success was justified by what is referred to as the Puritan ethic. This ethic stressed hard work and devotion to God, both of which were religiously mandated callings. Hard work, in effect, was a way of pleasing the Lord. Benjamin Franklin shifted the emphasis of the Puritan ethic in the direction of individual characteristics—frugality and effort—and lessened the religious emphasis somewhat, but not completely. The dual character and religious ethics predominated and were sharpened further by other ethic proponents in the nineteenth century. During this period the stewardship doctrine of wealth was also promulgated. This doctrine justified material success in terms of the responsibility of the wealthy (successful) to use their wealth for good purposes. Not everyone, however, agreed with this doctrine and some saw it frankly as a justification for greed. In the nineteenth century the Protestant ethic, which in many respects was a reformulation and reemphasis of the early colonial religion-based Puritan ethic, also prevailed.

As we came into the twentieth century, we certainly did not lack success ethics which could be used to justify material gains. The problem with these ethics was that they applied to relatively few people, some of whom became enormously wealthy and also heroes of their times. But the fact remained that most people were not responsive to these ethics, mostly because they weren't making much in the way of material gains.

In the 1930s there was a shift to another type of ethic, generally referred to as the personality ethic. The major stimuli for this ethic were the severely depressed economic conditions of the time, the need to find a way to make a living, and the publication of Dale Carnegie's book *How to Win Friends and Influence People* which showed people how they could earn a living by manipulating or trading on the motives and feelings of others. Basically, this book is a blatant form of manipulation

[7]Richard M. Huber, *The American Idea of Success.* New York: McGraw-Hill 1971.

which stresses how to get other people to do what you want them to do and to make them feel good in the process. Why then did large numbers of people seize upon it? For two reasons: it offered an easily learned skill and it worked. Many a manager and many a salesman owes his success to this approach, which, I might add, is still prevalent in our organizations today.

Regardless of the success ethic in vogue, every person, after he has achieved material success, becomes preoccupied with the question of what is the meaning of success. In other words, material success alone does not appear to be enough and the materially successful individual feels a need to deal with it in more philosophical terms. For our purposes, there is no need to go into all of the philosophical ramifications of what is true success, but suffice it to say that it is a problem which comes up in any success ethic.

Now, where are we today in terms of success, particularly in relation to the class of '67? There are a number of things we might say about them in this respect.

They come from an environment of material success and achieve it on their own relatively early in their lives. The class of '67 was raised in a period which perhaps represented the greatest material outpouring in our history. Not only was there a great outpouring of "things" (homes, autos, fashions) but there was an outpouring of things which one could do with surplus money, such as more leisure time. I think it would be fair to say that this group grew up without experiencing any significant material deficits as compared to those raised during the Depression or World War II.

In terms of Maslow's principles their material needs have been satisfied and therefore no longer are significant motivators for them. This is not to say that they are not interested in material things but that they have always had them and they can duplicate them easily when they strike out on their own. In other words, when they leave home they can easily replace the standard of living in which they were raised.

They are concerned with higher-order needs. In effect, the material pursuits of previous generations (particularly since 1945 when the class of '67 was born) have freed them from constraining material and economic concerns. With major medical and economic problems already solved, they are free to deal more with the higher-order needs of individual identity and growth—a luxury that no other generation in our society has had.

They may be rejecting the personality ethic. One of the subtler things that may be happening is the reaction of younger management employees to the personality ethic or the "management by manipulation" style. In very blunt terms they see this style as phony. A more sophisticated attribution is to refer to it as not being authentic. This reaction to the personality ethic probably is due to the usual intergenerational differences (the tendency of younger generations to reject the values of older generations) as well as the greater degree of openness and candor which generally characterize younger people. Many older managers have indicated that they feel uncomfortable with the candor shown by younger people. They are particularly uncomfortable when they are "forced" to expose their hidden agendas and to deal with problems in a more open and direct manner.

In all probability the next generation of middle managers will enter the middle management ranks at an earlier age than the managers they will replace. Those who do not move into top management positions, therefore, face the prospect of spending more years in the middle management ranks than their predecessors. This is another way of saying that they will have to cope with the middle management environment for longer periods of time. Over the long pull, how can we expect them to react? One possible reaction from the younger middle managers will be to spearhead the movement for manager unions. The previously cited AMA survey on manager unions showed that one-third of the then current middle managers between the age of 20 to 29 would join a union if one were organized in their company. Another 17 percent were uncertain, while 50 percent said no. This represents a fertile base in a group that will rapidly be taking over the middle management positions. While we cannot make flat-out predictions as to what they will do, we should keep in mind they either were involved participants or were firsthand observers to group action while they were on campus. In other words, they directly or indirectly experienced group action and have seen its results. They know what militancy can do.

Another crucial period for the class of '67 will be when they enter the midcareer phase. Previously, middle managers have coped through job and career changes, redirection of effort, or stagnation. But what about a generation that never had many economic hangups? How will they cope? They probably will react in the same way as the managers they are replacing—but even more so. We should anticipate more in the way of job changes, career changes, and redirection of effort. From the point of view of the organization, this will mean greater turnover in the middle management ranks and a less stable middle management population. Thus the group that top management looks to to implement their intentions may be an ever changing one which will put additional strains on the top executives.

In summary, the class of '67, the next generation of middle managers, is creating quite a bit of change and in all probability will continue to do so. The changes we have seen to date are of a quiet nature—increasing refusal to play the career ladder game and rejection of manipulative managerial styles. As for future changes, the class of '67 represents the leading edge for the potential of manager unions and for withholding their efforts from the organization through turnover and increased redirection of their efforts. Top management faces the prospect of an organized and highly mobile middle management population.

chapter six

Manager Dialogs I:
Organization Development

MANAGERS AT ALL LEVELS work in a complex environment. The complexities stem basically from differentiated roles, number of levels in the hierarchy, and sheer size of the organization. The top and middle managers, who constitute no more than 5 to 6 percent of the total workforce in the organization, must interrelate in a way to make the other 95 percent effective. In this chapter we will look at the interrelationships between the top and middle managers and among the middle managers themselves with a view toward creating greater understanding between these groups

VERTICAL RELATIONSHIPS

Mutual understanding is stressed because top managers and middle managers are apt to have quite different views of the organization, depending on their function and where they happen to be in the hierarchy. Thus top management may be concerned with the total goals of the organization, customers, government regulations, the financial community, various internal constituencies, and their own personal and financial stake in the organization. Middle managers, on the other hand, see the organization in terms of their more limited functional roles, the sets of relationships they have within and without the organization, and the specific goals and measurements which apply to them. Neither set of perceptions necessarily should be regarded as the "correct" one nor as having greater priority over the other. Both represent significant psychological facts of life for the beholders. What is important is for top and middle managers to be aware of and understand the other person's perceptions and not reject them out of hand as a defensive maneuver.

Defensive posturing takes place at all levels and in all directions.

Thus top management rationalizes its perceptions about middle management and vice versa; similarly, middle managers react defensively toward each other. Typically, organizations are rife with these reactions, which in turn become barriers against communication and cooperative effort.

The removal of these perceptual barriers is an important starting point in improving the situation of the middle managers. In top management –middle management relationships, the removal of the barriers would serve to eliminate and prevent the recurrence of the stereotyped images that develop between these groups. If this were the only result, then significant progress will have been achieved. However, removal of the barriers to a more open relationship will also give top and middle managers a more accurate picture of each other's needs and problems. It is imperative that top management understand the needs of the middle managers and that the middle managers understand the needs and constraints of top management. In other words, a climate of increased mutual understanding between the top and the middle is a prerequisite to meaningful change.

The perceptual barrier between the middle managers themselves needs to be reduced. As implementers of top management intentions and in their day-to-day role as coordinators, middle managers are highly interdependent. Stereotyped images of each other limit their personal effectiveness and the overall effectiveness of the organization. Gamesmanship and defensive posturing only distract from more constructive efforts.

The methods for dealing with the perceptual barriers involve special kinds of manager dialogs—some designed to bring the barriers down and others to minimize their recurrence. In particular, we are referring to organization development and goal-setting methods. The methods stemming from organization development are a means for examining and changing the quality of interpersonal relationships, while goal-setting methods provide one basis for maintaining improved day-to-day relationships. In this chapter we will describe organization development; Chapter 7 will deal with the goal-setting methods.

Organization development (OD) is a behavioral science based on a set of methods that basically deal with change. Warren Bennis, one of the leading OD advocates, defines organization development as ''a response to change, a complex educational strategy intended to change beliefs, attitudes, values, and structure of organizations so that they can better adapt to new technologies, markets, and challenges, and the dizzying rate of change itself.''[1] Bennis then states a number of charac-

[1]Warren Bennis, *Organization Development: Its Nature, Origins, and Prospects*. Reading, Mass.: Addison-Wesley, 1969.

teristics of the OD process. The relevant ones for this discussion are:

- OD is an educational strategy adopted to bring about a planned organizational change.
- The sought-after changes relate to important organization needs or problems.
- The OD educational strategy emphasizes the use of the experienced behavior of the participants.
- OD has specific goals which are of value to individuals and the organization: improved interpersonal relationships, better methods for resolving conflict, and increased mutual understanding.

Organizational development is a planned method for change. It deals with the past experiences of the individuals in the organization when setting the specific objectives that relate to important organization needs and problems. OD is not synonymous with sensitivity training, although sensitivity training could be part of the planned educational strategy if this particular method is considered appropriate. Nor should OD be regarded as similar to individual or group therapy. OD participants may find that they are called upon to deal openly with feelings about themselves and others (perhaps for the first time), but the intent is not so much to bring about personality changes as to show that feelings are part of the interpersonal agenda, that feelings do influence relations, and that people are capable of learning to deal with these feelings in a constructive way.

Let us consider two cases where OD was used within the context of this book. In the first case we shall show the use of OD to create better understanding and specific improvements in the relationship between top management (a new division general manager) and middle management. In the second case we will look at the use of OD in improving the lateral relationships among middle managers.

CASE 1: THE NEW DIVISION GENERAL MANAGER

BACKGROUND

This OD effort took place in a division of a large company. The division is a profit center with a distinct product line. A portion of the products was sold directly to industrial users. These products tended to be high priced and custom designed. Another portion of the product line was sold through distributors for ultimate use by individual consumers in their homes. The consumer products were standardized and mass produced.

For many years the division was very successful and had about 35 percent of the market. The division manager, who had been in place for 11 years, was not very demanding and quite paternalistic. He stressed a family approach to the business and took a strong personal interest in his staff. The management group under him was quite stable, with turnover mostly the result of retirement.

In 1969–1970 the business declined markedly. Costs rose sharply and new competitors took away one-third of their usual market. The division also had its first strike, which lasted almost seven weeks. The division manager was transferred to a corporate headquarters staff position and replaced by a person (from outside the division) with a strong financial background but with no managing experience in a line organization. He instituted a very detailed cost control system and attempted to introduce a standards system in the production area. His efforts met resistance in both the management and production ranks. He did not make much progress, and after one year, asked to be relieved of his assignment. He, in turn, was replaced by an experienced production manager (from outside the division) who left after three months to become a vice president of another company. The third division manager, again from outside the division, was young and ambitious and was regarded as having very high potential. His aspirations were to become president of the company, and he saw this situation as an opportunity to advance his career. His short-term goal was to turn this division around and move on. He made no secret of his ambitions or of his intentions.

During his first two months on the job, the new DGM asked for and received a great deal of information about business operations—costs, quality, delivery problems, and so on. During this period he established some high-priority items and made some minor organization and personnel changes. At the end of two months he felt he knew the business operations well enough to make his moves. At this point in time he saw himself as having several options:

1. He could "clean house" and bring in his own team.
2. He could work with the people already there.
3. Some combination of 1 and 2.

At this point, he engaged an outside consultant to review his alternatives and, in particular, to review the potential effects of these alternatives on the organization. After a lengthy discussion with the consultant, the DGM was able to sort out his own motives as follows:

● The turnaround of the division was important to him personally.

He wanted to do it in two years and felt that he could if he had a good management team working with him.

- His feelings about the current management team were mixed but inclined toward the negative. He saw them as unresponsive and needing a great deal of personal direction. However, he did respect their knowledge of the business.

- His preference was to work with the current management, but he felt that he had little rapport with them. He really seemed to be looking for a way to work with the present management if his basic objectives could be met, although he did not explicitly say so.

After some discussion with the consultant, the DGM agreed to some exploratory efforts that might lead to an OD effort to develop more rapport and teamwork within the current management. He made it clear that any OD effort would have to be acceptable to all the parties involved. He was not going to mandate it.

PROCEDURE

The consultant was introduced by the DGM to the management personnel at a group meeting. The DGM stated that he had asked the consultant to prepare a proposal as to how he (the consultant) could help the management group to work more effectively in dealing with its business problems. He made it clear that they would have an opportunity to reject or accept any proposal and that nothing would be done unless they consented. He asked for questions and comments and was greeted mostly by silence and several "safe" questions. After some additional explanation of how the proposal would be developed and the role they would play in its development, a low-key commitment to go through with the proposed activities resulted.

The consultant then arranged to meet privately with each manager for one to two hours. The interviewees were guaranteed anonymity and tended to be quite open and candid in the private interviews. They talked about the organization, its recent history, the new DGM, and what they felt had to be done to improve the organization. In summary, the following key issues emerged:

1. They respected the ability of the new DGM but were uncertain, and in some cases distrustful, of his motives and intentions. Some wondered what he was going to do with all the input he had received during the past two months, while others felt that he was sent in to turn the division around and that they might become the victims.

2. They felt that there was not enough teamwork, up and down or laterally, and that the rapid changes in leadership at the top had created

an 'every man for himself" situation. They wanted team effort. They also felt the division lacked direction.

3. They believed they were a competent and experienced group, and, if given an opportunity, they could make major contributions toward improving the performance of the division.

The results of the interviews were summarized and presented to the managers who were interviewed in a group session, which the DGM did not attend. After considerable discussion the managers agreed on the following: (1) They wanted to know more about the DGM and his intentions. They also felt he needed to know more about them personally and the specific problems they faced in doing their jobs. (2) The division needed a direction and a business plan.

The consultant then presented some OD methods that might address themselves to these needs. There was considerable discussion about the proposed methods, including questioning the desirability of such approaches. In the end, the managers agreed to a "team-building" session or a series of such sessions.[2] They did, however, feel that any initial confrontation with the DGM be done by three spokesmen from their group. In other words, they did not want to confront the DGM individually in a group session, nor did they want specific individual feedback from him about themselves. They felt that they had to approach him in "safer" ways at the outset until they got to know him better. The above approach was presented to the DGM by the three representatives of the management group, and after some minor questioning, he agreed to it.

The initial session was scheduled for one day. The meeting was opened by the consultant to set the stage. The three management representatives summarized the feelings of the managers regarding the DGM and the lack of direction in the division. The DGM then presented his views on the organization, its structure and needs. He was somewhat general in this presentation and did not refer to specific individuals or issues. The group then spent several hours in discussion.

As the discussion progressed, more and more managers participated and they became more specific. The DGM referred to problems in more detail and elaborated upon them; the managers also opened up in terms of their concerns. Some expressed strong resentment about their treatment in the past and the unnecessary poor reputation that they and the division had within the company.

Toward the end of the morning, the consultant summarized what the

[2]For a detailed description of team-building sessions, see J. K. Fordyce and R. Weil, *Managing with People*. Reading, Mass.: Addison-Wesley, 1971.

group had discussed and what appeared to be happening in the group—that they were now talking about real issues in a very direct and open way. The group discussed these observations for awhile and then agreed to meet in subgroups after lunch to come up with some refined statements of the needs of the organization and plans for future action. The afternoon session lasted until 7:00 PM. They had reached the following conclusions:

1. The one-day session cleared the air of a lot of concern and tension.

2. In general terms the managers and the DGM agreed that a business plan was needed to put the organization back on the road to becoming a successful business once more.

3. There was strong disagreement on the specifics of a recovery plan, and a feeling that more time was needed to develop one. A task force consisting of the DGM and a representative from each operating and staff function was designated and given the assignment of drawing up a business plan and presenting it to the group at a two-day meeting six weeks hence. The plan was to give appropriate emphasis to the short- and long-range actions that would help to turn the business around.

The second meeting came off on schedule. The planning task force actually was able to get copies of the plan to the managers for their review several days prior to the meeting. The meeting opened with a presentation by a member of the task force on how the plan was developed and an explanation of the strategy, intent, and content of the plan. His main purpose, at this point, was to insure understanding and not to deal with questions and objections.

The group was then subdivided into cross-functional teams. Each team critiqued the proposed recovery plan in detail and then reported their recommendations for change to the entire group. By the end of the first day, the group had agreed on a plan.

Starting on the evening of the first day and continuing through most of the morning of the second day, the group met in functional subgroups. Each functional team was asked to make detailed examination of the plan in light of what they had to do to make it succeed, the resources available to them, additional needs, and where they were highly dependent on other functions. Each functional team made a presentation to the total group, interspersed with considerable discussion.

Near the close of the second day, the group was asked to assess what they had accomplished. They responded that

• They now had a direction and a plan to help turn the business around.

• They were enthusiastic and optimistic.

- They were beginning to know the DGM and looked forward to working with him.
- They liked the group-planning session and suggested that they have a similar one quarterly to review progress and work out problems.
- They were receptive to the idea that some part of some of these meetings be devoted to additional OD efforts.

Quarterly group review and problem-solving sessions have now become an accepted routine in this organization and additional OD efforts have been made at these meetings.

COMMENTS

The significant breakthrough for this group came early in the first session as a result of the confrontation between the three management representatives and the DGM. The DGM, in particular, was quite candid in expressing his thoughts and in answering questions. His approach helped to overcome any fears about confronting the boss, and the group very quickly opened up.

Initial reticence about confronting the boss is not unusual, as quite often the managers are concerned about his "fate control" over them and how he might use it. In many instances some form of confrontation is needed to get things started. The actual form of the confrontation, however, has to be tailored to the situation. In this case, the managers used spokesmen. In other situations a consultant presents their views or feedback is made through questionnaires. Sometimes, the group prefers to confront the boss directly.

The enthusiasm and optimism of the group at the end of the second session visibly were quite high. However, these feelings can be transient and can lead to strong cynicism if not much happens as a result. The decision for follow-up meetings was important, as these sessions are the real test of the group's staying power and resolve. Planning sessions deal with the future, while follow-up sessions deal with results. The continuation of the OD effort in subsequent review and problem-solving sessions is very helpful to a group. It exposes them to a broader range of interpersonal skills, and, more importantly, in the context of real and at times significant business situations. This essentially was the approach that evolved with this division.

The division has made progress toward achieving its recovery plan, although it still has a way to go. The DGM has made some personnel changes, although he felt constrained to wait longer to do so than he might normally have. He is satisfied with the progress and feels that the OD has been helpful but not the sole factor that influenced their progress.

He and several corporate executives were quite impressed by the response of the management group to a later crisis which could have had serious negative consequences, and they felt that OD played a part in helping the management group to deal with the situation. The crisis involved the sudden and unexpected bankruptcy of a key and sole source supplier. This required a massive replanning effort to work around a parts shortage until a new vendor could start shipping parts. The management met over a weekend and came up with an alternate set of plans which they implemented on the following Monday morning. The management group knew their business plan and were committed to achieving it. They had had four quarterly review sessions prior to the crisis and were accustomed to working with each other in making changes. They moved into the crisis very well prepared in terms of knowledge and in ability to work with each other. The significant outcome was that they were able to come within 5 to 6 percent of their sales target through the replanning effort. They were now seen as a very flexible and adaptable group.

HORIZONTAL RELATIONSHIPS

Not all of the interpersonal problems encountered by middle managers are with persons higher up in the hierarchy. Many, if not most, of the problems middle managers have are with each other. The reasons for these difficulties stem from the nature of organization structure and the roles that the middle managers play in the structure. Typically, an organization is divided into functions, and, not uncommonly, middle managers identify strongly with their particular function and its values. Because their goals, both work and personal, are oriented toward their particular group, their loyalties tend to be more functional than organizational. The negative feelings, attitudes, and perceptions that result among the different groups have a way of becoming institutionalized and persisting over long periods of time. The result is mistrust and poor communications.

In the context of their functional loyalties and identifications, middle managers are expected to integrate work efforts across the organization. Here, again, they create problems for each other. In effect, each middle manager has a piece of the total work effort needed, and thus affect each other in many different ways. A maintenance manager can slow up the work of other middle managers if he is unresponsive and overly rigid in how he allocates his personnel; a components manufacturing manager can create havoc in the assembly if he does not meet his commitments; and support managers, such as in purchasing, can slow down the entire organization if they develop burdensome rules in order to maintain control over their own function.

To counteract these lateral interactions and the problems they create, middle managers develop ways of coping. The techniques they develop for dealing with each other sometimes are productive and sometimes not. Strauss[3] describes some of the tactics developed by middle managers in their lateral relationships:

Development of rules. Quite frequently, the demands that are made on a particular middle manager's organization become excessive, and he will try to develop some rules governing the input of work to his organization. This is common in service functions such as purchasing, maintenance, and data processing. For example, purchasing may stipulate a 30-day lead time for certain types of material requests. Generally, these rules can be helpful in avoiding panic efforts and other disruptions in the servicing organization. The difficulty is that they can also become a problem to the middle manager who desperately and genuinely needs the particular service. This is where the fun usually begins. If the servicing organization is overly rigid in the face of genuine need, then conflict and bad feelings are generated. The manager who needs the service may try to exert leverage to "force" the servicing manager to respond. The matter may be appealed to persons upward in the hierarchy and a decision made there. No matter who wins in this confrontation, there is a net residue of negative feelings, attitudes, and perceptions. If this is a common occurrence, then the negative aspects can build up rapidly and persist.

Evasion of rules. Just as some managers are prone to develop rules to facilitate the functioning of their organization, other managers become adept at evading rules to get what they need. They may go around, through, above, or below the organization from which they need something, but they will find a way of evading a rule when they feel they have to do so to meet their goals. Rule evasion can produce negative effects. Quite frequently, the manager who evades a rule is doing so at the expense of some other manager who is an innocent party to the entire transaction. Also, the manager whose rule has been evaded will probably develop negative feelings. At best, his self-esteem might be temporarily reduced; at worst, he may decide that he needs tighter rules and a better vigilance system. Most likely, he will start to develop a

---

[3]George Strauss, "Tactics of Lateral Relationship," *Administrative Science Quarterly* (September 1962), pp. 161–186.

healthy distrust and dislike for other managers who try to go around him. Again, these feelings can accumulate and persist over long periods of time.

"Old boy" network. Many middle managers recognize their inter-dependencies and trade favors with each other. They rely on friendships and favors with the clear recognition that there is a time to give and a time to get. This, of course, is the informal organization at its best. The only problem that arises here is for the middle managers who, for some reason, do not get into the network.

Education. Middle managers, particularly of service organizations, quite frequently find it valuable to educate other middle managers about their function. A data processing center manager can point out how the center operates, the type of equipment that is available, the service that is being offered, the limitations on the service, and how the actions of operating managers can help or hinder the operation of the data processing facility. Quite frequently, this approach results in better work relationships. It also offers the users of the service an opportunity to express their dissatisfactions and to stimulate needed improvements.

Organization interaction tactics. Tactics that develop between organizations can be either facilitative or nonfacilitative. For example, a facilitative tactic is to check first with another organization before making an unusual or demanding request of it. In other words, give them time to get ready and perhaps to come up with some alternatives. A nonfacilitative tactic is to try to take over a troublesome or unresponsive organization through organization changes. This, of course, may eliminate problems for the organization doing the taking over, but it may not improve things for other organizations who require its cooperation.

As can be seen, the tactics that middle managers develop can be helpful, not helpful, or even make the situation worse. OD methods have been found to be useful when the negative aspects of the situation have become institutionalized. In these situations OD efforts typically deal with the past by dissipating its effects in the present, thus laying the groundwork for more constructive interpersonal relationships in the future. The following case is illustrative.

CASE 2: SALES VERSUS PRODUCTION

BACKGROUND

One of the significant characteristics of successful printing firms is their ability to provide service to their customers. This means a willingness on the part of the printing company to meet unanticipated demands, considerable last-minute efforts to meet shipping deadlines, responsiveness to customer changes, and the rescheduling of work and priorities to satisfy customers.

The need to provide service frequently creates strain and conflict between the sales and production departments. The salesmen often feel that they are not getting the service from production to satisfy their customers and that the shop does not keep them well enough informed of problems. The production people quite frequently are caught between the conflicting demands of different salesmen and are trying to complete orders with insufficient information or are unsure as to what the customer wants.

In one company (80 employees; very strong sales and service orientation; technically progressive, talented, and ambitious top management team), there was evidence of friction between sales and production. The company president talked about the lack of integration in his management team; the sales manager complained about the lack of timely feedback from the shop about problems; and the production manager talked about incomplete specifications, overly aggressive salesmen, and last-minute orders and changes which resulted in inefficiencies. Shop employees were interviewed and it was apparent that they were affected by the top management conflicts. They tended to become indifferent when too many jobs were labeled "rush." At times, quality slipped and errors were made as a result of efforts to meet crash deadlines.

As a result of these initial explorations, a proposal was made to the management team to conduct problem-solving or team-building sessions. The purposes of the sessions would be to "mend the fences" between departments, to get at the causes of problems which keep the company from being more effective than it already is, and to develop solutions for any other problems that may be uncovered.

PROCEDURE

The key managers agreed to participate in a team-building and group problem-solving process and were given the following instructions several weeks prior to the session:

1. Select a key person in your department to work with you now and to attend the problem-solving session with you.
2. Meet with this person and establish a method for identifying those things which keep your department from being more effective. Here are some suggested questions:

- Where do we fall down as an organization? Why?
- Who are the people with whom we have the most trouble? Why?
- If we could change one thing around here, what would it be?
- Who do we have the most trouble understanding?
- With whom do we have the most trouble communicating?
- How good are our systems and procedures?
- What are the persistent problems we have in getting our work done?

3. Summarize the answers to the above questions. Be specific—name names, give reasons, and cite examples. Put this material on flip charts and be prepared to make a 20- to 30-minute presentation to the entire group.

The group prepared their presentations and attended a session away from the plant where the following agenda was followed:

1:00	PM	Introduction
1:10	PM	Observations of the organization made by the consultant
1:30	PM	Team presentations of problems
3:30	PM	Break
4:00	PM	Discussion and summary of problem
6:00	PM	Dinner
7:30	PM	Development of solutions and action plans
9:30	PM	Adjourn

In addition to the above agenda, these two ground rules were established for the session:

1. There were to be no rebuttals to any of the presentations. They were at the meeting to listen and to try to understand the other person's point of view. They were not here to defend themselves. This ground rule was established to prevent the session from becoming an argumentative gripe session. While rebuttals were not completely eliminated, they were kept to a minimum. As a result, "listening" was increased.

2. Each person must be prepared to contribute to solutions regardless of what may have been said about his organization. This ground rule was established to emphasize the participation in problem solving that would be needed if the group was to come up with meaningful answers.

In general, the ground rules were followed and presentations were thoughtful, well organized, and complete.

RESULTS

After the team presentations, the management participants discussed the many problems that were listed and identified the most significant ones:

Order Inputs

Many of the problems had to do with the way sales orders came to the organization. Two major items emerged in this category.

Where does work come into the organization? After some discussion it became clear that work orders were coming into the organization in two different places. Some jobs come first to the art department while others went first to the production department. In either case, one of the departments was not always aware of all the jobs that were in process. At times an unknown job caught them by "surprise" and seriously affected their schedules.

Quality of customer specifications. There was general agreement that the quality of customers' specifications created many problems. At times, jobs were started knowingly with incomplete specifications. In many of these instances, the specifications were not completed on a timely basis and errors resulted. In other cases, the specifications were incomplete because of poor salesman discipline.

Communications

Communications emerged as a significant problem in the organization, particularly face-to-face communication related to the day-to-day operations and priorities of the business. Two major items emerged from this category.

Day-to-day coordination. One of the significant problems identified by the group was the lack of day-to-day coordination on the many changes and shifts in scheduling and priority which normally occur in a service-oriented business. The group accepted the need to make these changes but agreed that they did not have an effective means of communicating and coordinating them.

Communications to shop employees. The staff group felt that employees did not understand the reasons for many of the things they were asked to do and this partly accounted for the indifference shown by some shop employees. They also recognized that they had to communicate better among themselves before they could improve their communications to employees.

Systems and Procedures

The company already had systems and procedures that could solve some of the problems, but they were not being used or coordinated well.

Organization Structure

This problem had to do with the organization structure, reporting relationships, and authority that staff members felt they had. The issue centered about the fact that one staff member wore "two hats" (vice president of the company and sales manager). The two hats role was not entirely clear to him and other staff members—when was he acting as vice president and when was he acting as sales manager? The company president dealt with this issue on the spot in a very candid manner and was able to satisfy the staff members. The resolution of this issue, which had been bothering people, could be looked upon as a "bonus" from the team-building effort.

The group then spent several hours coming up with specific solutions for the problems.

1. Establish a sales service correspondent position in the production department to handle all incoming orders. This person would write and control the distribution of orders in the shop. In addition, he would follow up to get complete information for the specifications when needed.

Through the discussion, it became apparent that the position of sales service correspondent would be an important one and that a high-caliber person would be needed to deal effectively with salesmen in the field as well as people in the production department. In addition, the group saw considerable value in using the job of assistant sales correspondent as a training position for young potential salesmen. Thus, as a result of developing a solution for controlling orders, they also came up with a more effective training program.

2. Establish a brief daily meeting at a fixed hour to communicate about the more immediate and pressing scheduling and production problems. This daily meeting would be concerned about "yesterday, today, and tomorrow," and would be attended by the art director, heads of shipping, type, pressroom, bindery, production control, and the production manager. Any coordination that was needed would take place in this meeting. Any information that needed to be passed on to employees could be gotten from this meeting.

3. The group assigned the responsibility for systems and procedures to the production control organization. They would be responsible for updating, implementing, and monitoring these systems.

COMMENTS

The net result of the meeting was a statement of specific solutions to specific problems raised by the group. The problems dealt with by the group were of long standing and the solutions for some of them were not particularly complex. In fact, some of the solutions had been proposed prior to the meeting and not acted upon by the organization. Why then did it take a session of this type to get the problems and solutions identified, and what makes a meeting like this effective? There are a number of factors involved.

1. The meeting was considered to be important. Staff members were asked to prepare for a presentation prior to the meeting. The meeting was held away from the plant and away from the day-to-day work pressures.

2. All of the participants were affected by the problems that were brought up. Although they were affected in different ways, each staff member expressed some concern and frustration about the way these problems were affecting his department. In short, they were ready to find solutions.

3. The meeting established a climate for candor. The participants dealt with important issues and leveled with each other about basic causes. Although the president of the company was unexpectedly put in a position of answering questions about organization structure, job relationships, and authority, he responded candidly to the questions—further contributing to the openness with which problems were discussed. Personalities did not emerge as an issue in this group, although in some situations they were part of the problems facing the group.

4. This group was innovative and willing to experiment. Creativity and experimentation are a part of their work and they very willingly agreed to try an approach they had not used before. In order to use these methods effectively, an experimental and open-minded approach is imperative.

OD encompasses a wide range of methods with many useful applications in organizations. The two cases we have cited stress methods that deal with the past history between individuals and different parts of an organization. Emphasis has been on this aspect as a means of illustrating the use of OD because the past history probably represents, in most situations, the greatest single barrier for progress in solving the problems in the middle management organization. Our past experience with others tends to be with us in the present and colors our perceptions and interpretations of people and situations. Thus, if a top executive has developed a perception that middle managers are unresponsive, then this becomes his "set," or tendency to view middle managers in a particular way. Not only does the perception predispose him to see middle managers in a certain way, but he may then relate to the middle managers in an unconstructive way because of the predisposition.

Middle managers, of course, have fixed perceptions of top executives and of each other, which in turn further cloud the relationships within an organization. The important value and need for OD at the outset is to break through these perceptual sets and help to reestablish interpersonal relationships on a more realistic basis.

chapter seven

Manager Dialogs II:
Goal Setting and Performance Review

IN THE PRECEDING chapter, we discussed the use of organization development as a way to overcome interpersonal problems and to create a more constructive interpersonal climate. In this chapter we consider the use of another set of dialogs—goal setting and performance—which relates more specifically to the day-to-day work and ongoing business of the organization.

Goal-setting and performance-review methods, commonly referred to as management by objectives (MBO), are gaining wide recognition and acceptance as a valuable management tool. Some of the many important advantages of goal-setting methods that account for their growing acceptance follow:

Provide for a greater unity of direction. Organizations tend to be goal oriented. Typically, goals are established at the top management levels for the entire organization and in theory "cascade" downward and engage the attention and energies of persons at lower organization levels. Formal goal-setting processes at all levels in the organization help to insure that everyone is pulling in the same direction.

Help to clarify organization and individual roles. As indicated in earlier chapters, as organizations grow they tend to differentiate, that is, subdivide into more and more functions and become more complex. The tendency toward increased differentiation and complexity, in turn, increases the need to insure that there is a method in place that will adequately inform all employees and segments in the organization about their roles. Goal-setting methods, if used appropriately, have the potential to provide this information.

Provide feedback about performance. Feedback has many important uses. For the organization, it provides a measure of progress and important signals for the need for additional or corrective action relative to specific goals. For the person, it satisfies the important human need of knowing how one is doing. Performance feedback also gives the organization measurement data that can be used as a basis for improvement planning and for rewarding performance.

There is no question that more extensive involvement of top executives and middle managers in goal-setting and performance-review activities would be beneficial to the top executives, the middle managers, and the total organization as a whole. Goal-setting methods offer an opportunity for "one-on-one" dialogs that can only increase mutual understanding and performance results. We will address ourselves in this chapter to how middle managers can use goal-setting methods to achieve constructive results. We will stress the behavioral aspects of goal-setting and performance-review methods as opposed to their procedural aspects, which have received adequate attention by others.[1-3]

By behavioral aspects, we mean the following:

1. Characteristics of the goal-setting and performance-review process that affect the success of these activities. In this category are included the characteristics of goals, the number of goals, and the frequency of reviews.
2. Sociopsychological aspects of the goal-setting and performance-review process and their effects on the process. In this category are included participation, the effects of criticism and praise, and personal characteristics of the superior and the subordinate.

The distinction is made between the procedural and behavioral aspects of goal-setting and performance-review methods because we think this distinction is critical to the success of these types of programs. Goal-setting methods, from a strict procedural point of view, are nothing more than a series of logical and rational steps to be taken in planning. The content can be quite precise because the operations of an organization involve a lot of detail.

In effect, the logic of goal-setting methods is that, if everyone knows what is expected of him and does what is expected of him, then the planned-for results will be obtained. The fact is, we don't always get the results for which we planned. For some, this is a signal to go back

[1]G. Odiorne, *Management by Objectives.* New York: Pitman, 1964.
[2]J. W. Humble, *How to Manage by Objectives.* AMACOM, 1973.
[3]Paul Mali, *Managing by Objectives.* New York: Wiley, 1972.

and apply the procedures more intensively; for others it is a signal to abandon the process. In addition to understanding and implementing the goal-setting procedures, we also need to know and to take into account how individuals react to such a process and then to change the process to be more compatible with human reactions—hence, the emphasis on the behavioral aspects of goal-setting and performance-review processes. The advantages of goal-setting and performance-review processes are significant enough to take the time to learn about behavioral considerations and to use this information in a *constructive* manner. If the behavioral aspects are ignored, then we can confidently predict that many MBO programs will not reach their full potential and that many others will fail and be abandoned.

We will deal with the behavioral aspects of goal-setting and performance-review processes as they apply to middle managers in two steps. In the first step we will put goal setting and performance review into perspective by examining the evolution of the knowledge pertinent to the relevant behavioral factors, much of which comes from the study of performance-appraisal methods. In the second step we will examine in detail the procedures involved in goal setting and performance review and point the relevant behavioral considerations at each step.

GOAL SETTING AND PERFORMANCE REVIEW IN PERSPECTIVE

Many of the problems found in goal-setting methods are simply problems that derive from traditional appraisal systems. The trouble with appraisal systems is that they tend to be multipurpose and the purposes conflict with each other. The nature of these conflicts can be seen by reviewing some of the research that has been done on appraisal.

APPRAISAL

Douglas McGregor,[4] in a classic article, gave some of the first insights as to what was happening in the appraisal interview and why appraisal systems were failing. He pointed out that managers were very uncomfortable in the role of the appraiser. They did not like "to play God." They rejected or resisted in various ways the notion of sitting down with a valued employee and giving him negative feedback and then having to deal with the reactions of the employee. The employee, on the other hand, resented the process, particularly if it dealt with personal characteristics, as so many of our appraisal systems did and still do.

[4]Douglas McGregor, "An Uneasy Look at Performance Appraisal," *Harvard Business Review* (May-June 1957), pp. 89–94.

In 1958, Norman Maier of the University of Michigan published a book based on role-playing sessions involving different types of performance-appraisal discussions.[5] Maier found that both the manager and the subordinate have trouble with the interview. The manager, in effect, was in a conflicting role. He was being asked to play the roles of both helper and judge, and was resorting to various techniques to help him through the situation. For example, Maier referred to the manager's use of the "sandwich technique." Using this technique, the manager attempted to overcome the negative reactions of the employee to criticism by "sandwiching" the criticism between praise. An example of the sandwich technique might be an interview that starts this way:

> Jones, it's time for us to review your performance again and I'd like to start out by telling you what a pleasure it has been to have someone like you in our organization. You have a good attitude, you work hard, you're punctual, you're very conscientious but...

What follows the "but" is a criticism, and after the criticism the manager will come back very quickly with more praise. The employee, on the other hand, was not responding in the appraisal interview in the manner in which the manager hoped he would. The employee was not accepting criticism in a positive manner and giving indications that he was going to correct or improve his performance. Rather the employee was rejecting the manager's criticism by being defensive. He denied what the manager said; blamed other people; and gave excuses for his performance.

Research in the General Electric Company[6] supported Maier's findings about role playing. In the GE study managers and employees were observed as the actual appraisal was conducted. The observer coded the interview in terms of the amount of criticism and praise given by the manager, as well as the reactions of the employees. As was the case in Maier's study employees were defensive and managers used the sandwich technique. A major recommendation from both Maier's and the General Electric studies was to split the manager's roles in performance appraisal by having the manager conduct different types of appraisals for different purposes at different times. In particular, they greatly emphasized the separation of day-to-day discussions of performance (helper role) from summary discussions, which are an attempt to justify salary or other reward decisions (judge role).

[5]N. R. F. Maier, *The Performance Appraisal Interview: Objectives, Methods and Skills.* New York: Wiley, 1958.
[6]H. H. Meyer, E. Kay, and J. R. P. French, Jr., "Split Roles in Performance Appraisal," *Harvard Business Review* (January-February 1965), pp. 123–129.

In spite of what has been learned about the performance-appraisal process, it does not appear, even today, that the expectations of appraisal systems are being met; and it also does not appear that the frustrations in the use of appraisals are any lower than they have been in the past. The problem lies in the fact that we have not put into practice what we have learned about the appraisal process. There is no doubt that better results could be obtained if greater attention were paid to the following factors:

Clarification of the objectives of appraisal. Appraisal serves many purposes—manpower planning, manpower development, job understanding, compensation—and it is important that, initially, the *specific* purposes be identified. Once the basic question of appraisal for what has been answered, we can proceed to the consideration of the remaining important factors.

Appropriate techniques for each appraisal purpose. Once the objectives of appraisal have been identified, then a technique for each appraisal purpose can be constructed. Different appraisal purposes require different methods. For example, an appraisal of an individual's potential for a high-level managerial position is quite different in technique from an appraisal of his day-to-day job performance.

Clarification of the superior's role. Many appraisal systems stress the superior's role as a helper or a judge and tend to intermix these roles. The result is that the role of the judge tends to predominate and cancel out the potential benefit of his role as a helper. The emphasis on the judge role also creates considerable discomfort in the superior and, as a result, he tends to avoid appraisal situations. Appraisal systems should be designed to avoid the conflicting role and to increase the superior's opportunities to be in the role of a helper. There are legitimate situations where the superior should give emphasis to his judgmental role, and while these situations are important, they tend to be infrequent, for example, the annual salary review. There is no reason why these infrequent judgmental situations should overpower and negate the far more frequent opportunities the superior has for acting in the more useful helper role.

Expansion of the subordinate's role. The typical appraisal system tends to put the subordinate into a passive role. He pretty much sits and listens to what his boss has to say. In situations where he is being judged, he has almost no alternative but to become defensive. Silence, of course, is another alternative. Use of goal-setting and performance-review methods should be encouraged, as they enable the subordinate to become a more active participant.

PROCEDURES

If we were to look at the appraisal methods with the above factors in mind, we would come up with the following appraisal procedures.

Manpower Planning

Objectives. The objectives of manpower planning are *(a)* to identify future manpower needs, *(b)* to establish requirements for key positions, *(c)* to assess the potential of individuals for critical positions, and *(d)* to identify career paths and other development activities that will insure development of employees for key positions.

Relevant techniques. The appraisal part of manpower planning basically requires techniques that can predict the potential performance of an individual. A common technique for assessing this potential is for the manager to make a judgment. Typically, the superior is asked to estimate the organization level or higher-level position in which the subordinate could perform adequately and when the subordinate might be ready to assume such a position.

For several reasons the validity of this nomination procedure is doubtful. First, there is the matter of the superior's motivation. He may not want to nominate an exceptionally good employee for fear of losing him. Or he may nominate an individual to get "off the hook" and to demonstrate his good intentions to employees. If the employee subsequently is not promoted, the manager can at least say that he tried. Second, and more important, the manager may know little or nothing about the requirements of the position for which he is nominating the subordinate. Even if his intentions are good, he may wind up nominating the wrong person.

Assessment centers are a more valid alternative to the manager nomination technique. This method consists of evaluating the individual by observing his performance in various exercises which simulate the higher-level positions he is being considered for. In effect, the exercises are job samples. In spite of the fact that they increase the visible costs for evaluation, assessment centers are being increasingly used because of the validity of their results.[7]

Superior's role. Use of assessment centers will diminish the superior's role in appraising potential, as well it should. However, the superior will still be called upon to nominate individuals as candidates for assess-

[7]For more on assessment centers, see W. C. Byham, "Assessment Centers for Spotting Future Managers," *Harvard Business Review* (July-August 1970), pp. 150–160.

ment. He can be helped in this role by being provided with more information about the position requirements. The problems of the superior's motivation can be alleviated by allowing employees to nominate themselves subject to additional screening by the personnel department against position requirements.

Subordinate's role. There are a number of ways to actively involve the subordinate in the manpower planning process. First, he can test his ambition against the positions that might be available to him in the organization. Are these the types of positions he wants? What does he have to do to become qualified? Is he willing to do and endure what has to be done in order to qualify? Second, he can become more active in planning and carrying out the actions that might qualify him. Too often, employees are kept in the dark about possible opportunities and the necessary steps they must take to meet the requirements.

Day-to-Day Job Performance

Objectives. To provide the subordinate with *(a)* an understanding of his position requirements, *(b)* the specific goals associated with his position, and *(c)* feedback about his job performance.

Relevant techniques. Every exempt employee should have a job description which lists his basic responsibilities and the general areas of measurement for these responsibilities. The job description is a relatively static document and should change infrequently.

The goal-setting method is the core of the day-to-day job activities and is the best available method for creating a mutual understanding of the work the subordinate should be doing. Periodic reviews of goals provide performance feedback to the subordinate relative to his efforts. They are conducted with a view toward helping the employee better understand what is expected of him and to provide him with help in solving job-related problems.

Superior's role. Goal-setting and performance-review methods offer the superior his greatest opportunities to project himself into the helper role. During the process of setting goals, the superior can help the subordinate to achieve higher levels of job understanding. In addition, he can be helpful in setting priorities and in developing strategies and identifying resources that will help the subordinate to achieve his goals. During the performance-review sessions, the superior can engage in constructive problem solving with the subordinate in those areas where his progress is lagging.

Subordinate's role. Goal-setting and performance-review processes offer the subordinate opportunities for a more active role in planning his work, in reviewing his performance, and in solving work-related problems that will help him to be more effective.

Development Planning

Examination of appraisal methods shows that little attention is given to development planning, and the roles of the manager and the employee tend to be obscure. In the typical appraisal the manager is asked to indicate the career interests of the employee and the necessary steps for the employee to take in order to achieve those ambitions. Usually the recommendations run along the lines of taking a course or reading a book or getting rid of an undesirable personality characteristic.

Development planning requires much more information about the subordinate and the work situation. In addition, it needs to be supported with appropriate formats and policies. The following are important methods for development planning.

● Statement of personal goals. Each employee should have an opportunity to state and evaluate his personal goals in the organization.

● Position information. To do realistic development planning, the employee should have access to information about positions in the organization: He should have an opportunity to learn about position requirements, the frequency with which certain positions become available, and the location of positions in which he might have some interest.

● Evaluation data. The subordinate should have access to evaluation data about himself that he can use in planning his development. If he has been tested he should have a feedback session on the test results from a professionally qualified person. If he has been through an assessment center, then he should have a feedback session geared toward helping him understand his development needs. If his performance has been summarized on an annual or periodic basis, then these summaries should be available to him. In other words, provide the subordinate with enough information about *himself* so he can do some realistic development planning.

● Career paths. Career paths should be designated, particularly for higher-level positions. The career paths should provide the experiences and on-the-job testing that are necessary for advancement or that make for a well-rounded manager. The boxing in of many middle managers, in effect, is caused by the fact that they have advanced through narrow functional career paths.

● Development policies and practices. Development planning activities should be supported by appropriate organization policies and practices. There are several that are basic:

1. There usually is a need for a policy that establishes the development planning process. This policy should define the process and relate it to other activities such as manpower planning and goal setting.

2. There usually is a need for a policy dealing with interdivisional moves and cross-functional training. This is a particularly important area in that interdivisional and cross-functional moves are important elements in the career paths that lead to well-rounded middle managers. This also is an area where strong resistances are encountered and, frankly, a well-enforced policy can be of great value.

3. There is a need for policies dealing with the development planning for mature or plateaued employees. This is a neglected area and should deal with such matters as cross-functional training, sabbaticals for education, preparation for second careers (in or out of the employing organization), and preparation for earlier retirement. The next chapter deals with these matters in more detail.

Objectives. To provide the employee with the stimulation and opportunity to develop his current job skills and to prepare for advancement to the extent that it is appropriate and reflects the interests of the individual.

Relevant techniques. Stress is placed on development planning as opposed to career planning because development planning should be the more prevalent activity. Career planning is more appropriate for individuals who have a good shot at top jobs in the organization. For most middle managers the facts of life are that their careers will plateau at just about where they are in the organization. As an individual is promoted up through the hierarchy, the odds against future promotions become prohibitively high and the individual therefore must focus on development *within his current job.* The stress on career planning for those few who might make it to the top has resulted in neglect of development planning for the majority who might pursue useful careers in the middle of the organization.

Subordinate's role. In development planning the order of the discussion of the superior's and subordinate's role is reversed because we see the subordinate as having more of the initiative in this process. The superior is primarily the helper.

The subordinate's role in development planning should be significantly increased by having *him* play a major part in assessing his current abilities and in developing plans for his growth and the means by which these plans will be achieved. In other words, techniques of self-appraisal are appropriate to the development planning process. The subordinate can be helped in development planning in several ways. He should be given a series of searching questions about himself to answer. In other words, his first action is to take a hard look at himself:

1. What have I accomplished thus far in my career which can be regarded as significant accomplishments, and why?
2. What have I not accomplished in my career thus far which might be regarded as significant failures, and why?
3. Based on this analysis (answers to questions 1 and 2), what do I regard as my strengths and weaknesses?
4. To what jobs in the organization do I aspire?
   (a) What are the requirements for these jobs?
   (b) How qualified am I at the present time for these positions?
   (c) What will I have to do in order to have a reasonably good chance of achieving these positions?
   (d) To what extent am I willing and able to do what is necessary to qualify for one of these positions?
5. What do I regard as the significant accomplishments and lack of accomplishments in my present position, and why?
   (a) What can I do in my present position to capitalize on my strengths?
   (b) What specific actions should I be taking in order to overcome areas of poorer performance?

These kinds of questions put more of the responsibility for development planning on the individual and also permit a better balance between development on one's present job and planning for the future where it is appropriate to do so.

As is evident from the questions, the subordinate and the manager will need considerably more information about the job to which the subordinate aspires. Thus they both should be provided with information that will make the planning more realistic. For example, they should have information about the job requirements for the positions to which the employee might aspire; he should know about the demands that his goals will make on him. This information might come from the same data that is developed to help the manager in assessing potential, or it might come from the manpower development specialist in the organization, who, in effect, should be a resource for every person and for every job in the organization.

Superior's role. The superior's role in the development planning process is to review with the employee the inputs that the subordinate made to the development plan as described above. Here, again, the superior's role is one of a helper. He can help the subordinate get information about the requirements and to understand what these requirements mean and how they relate to performance on his present job, and he can also direct the employee into areas where the subordinate may not have looked. The self-appraisal also gives the superior a more realistic basis for suggestions to the subordinate. For example, if the subordinate has a development plan which is wholly unrealistic, either overly ambitious or underly ambitious, then at a minimum the manager knows where the employee is and can take it from there.

Manager and employee should have a formal development planning session at least once a year. They can then make reviews during the year to see what progress is being made, to analyze various problems or roadblocks, to contribute new inputs about job requirements, opportunities, and so on—all basically to help the employee achieve the goals that he has set for himself.

Performance Summaries and Justification for Rewards

Objectives. To provide the subordinate with an annual summary of his status in the organization and to provide the organization with a documented record of his performance.

Relevant techniques. There are two methods that are useful to meet the objectives. One method is the *annual performance summary*. This is a summary of the individual's performance as reflected in the achievement or nonachievement of his day-to-day performance. In effect, it summarizes the periodic performance reviews conducted as part of the goal-setting and performance-review process. A typical format for recording this summary is shown in Figure 3. As can be seen, no provision is made for ratings, deliberately so, as ratings do not contribute much to the appraisal process. If anything they tend to interfere as the superior is called upon to justify ratings, which in turn leads to defensiveness by the subordinate. Also, ratings are never fully used by managers. Approximately 80 to 85 percent of subordinates typically are rated on two points of scale. In other words, the ratings do not reflect the relative value of subordinates. For these reasons, it is recommended that ratings not be used. The annual performance summary should become a document for the record.

The second method is the annual salary review. Each exempt employee should have his salary reviewed annually and be provided with some justification for the current salary decision. Typically, this is the most difficult appraisal discussion for managers. There are, however, a number of things that can help the superior in this situation:

1. If he engages in goal-setting and performance-review sessions throughout the year, then a negative salary decision should not come

3. Format for a summary appraisal.

ANNUAL SUMMARY APPRAISAL

NAME _____

POSITION TITLE _____

ORGANIZATION _____

A. *Summary of Performance* (This commentary should reflect the manager's judgment about specifics such as achievements versus work plans/goals, effectiveness in supporting component goals, timeliness of performance, integration with others, and supervision required.)

   1. *Significant accomplishments:*

   2. *Areas where accomplishment fell short of expectations:*

B. Describe the strengths that are reflected in the employee's performance which contribute to his effectiveness on the job and should contribute to his development.

C. Describe the factors that are reflected in the employee's performance which limit his effectiveness on the job and may tend to hinder his development.

D. Describe immediate needs for improving current performance and/or increasing potential for assuming greater responsibility and list actions to be taken.

Appraiser's Signature _____Date_____

Reviewer's Signature_____Date_____

Date of Discussion with Employee_____

Copies: Employee's folder, employee (optional)

---

as too great a surprise to the subordinate. The surprise effect at salary review time is quite instrumental in producing defensiveness in subordinates.

2. The superior is helped in salary discussions if the organization has a salary system which is equitable and administered according to the rules. In other words, both the superior and the subordinate need to have confidence that they are dealing with a good system.

3. The superior must know enough about the salary system to discuss it meaningfully with the subordinate. At a minimum, the superior should know the salary ranges from various levels of jobs so he can point out to the subordinate what the financial opportunities are for him, the general methods by which jobs are evaluated so he can explain the basis for the subordinate's evaluation to him, and the philosophy of pay as it relates to performance so that he can discuss the factors which influence. Far too often, this type of information is withheld from the superior. The lack of such information not only lessens the superior's personal confidence in the system, but it also makes it more difficult for him to justify salary decisions to subordinates. The annual salary review also becomes a document for the record.

Superior's role. In the case of the annual performance summary, the superior's role is one of contributing input. Depending on his preference, the superior can (*a*) write the annual performance summary and review it with the subordinate, (*b*) get input from the subordinate and then write the summary, (*c*) or have the subordinate write it and then edit it. There does not seem to be any preferred way of writing such a summary.

In the case of the annual salary review, the manager probably will be required to write it as a matter of policy. The superior should clearly identify those factors which have influenced the pay decision. These typically include performance, marketplace value of the job, trend of performance, business conditions and ability of the organization to give increases, and where in the salary range the subordinate's current salary is. The manager should discuss the reasons with the subordinate in a straightforward manner stating the reasons for the decision.

In discussing poor performance, the superior may want to emphasize the areas for performance where improvement might lead to consideration for future increases. For the subordinate who is at or near the top of his salary range, the superior should point this out as a feature of the system and perhaps explore ways the subordinate might prepare himself for a promotion to a position in a higher salary range. The worst possible thing a superior can do in a salary discussion, particularly in a negative one, is to shift the blame for the decision onto someone else. Words to the effect that "I put you in for a bigger increase but someone upstairs did not approve it" is a transparent cop-out of the first order which lessens the confidence of the subordinate in the superior's authority.

Subordinate's role. The subordinate plays an active role in the preparation of the annual performance summary. He can contribute to it or write it, subject to some editing by his superior. The advantages of employee involvement are that some of the secretiveness of the process is eliminated and it helps to insure that the summary will be seen as fair to him.

We have gone to great lengths to put goal setting and performance review in perspective in terms of a variety of appraisal needs and processes. Several important points emerge from this review:

1. There are several distinct objectives in which appraisal plays a key role. In our review we have identified four objectives—manpower planning, day-to-day job performance, development planning, and performance summaries and justification for rewards. The objectives are important to both the organization and the employees and involve a variety of activities other than appraisal. In other words, appraisal is not an end in itself, but has distinctive and important uses in supporting various objectives.

2. Different appraisal methods and superior-subordinate roles are needed to support the different objectives. In our analysis we have seen that a variety of valid appraisal methods are needed to support various objectives. Among those discussed are assessment centers, periodic reviews, which possibly involve self-appraisal by subordinates, self-evaluation as part of development planning, narrative summary appraisals, and summary appraisals to justify salary decisions.

These appraisal methods require the superior and subordinate to play various roles. In manpower planning and annual salary review, the superior is cast mostly in the role of the judge and is asked to justify various decisions to the subordinate or others. In day-to-day goal setting, development planning, and annual performance planning, the superior has distinct opportunities to act as a helper to the subordinate. We also see opportunities for the subordinate's role to change from a passive to a more active one. Thus there are many more opportunities for both the superior and the subordinate to be involved in the appraisal process.

3. Appraisal methods should be designed and used to avoid or minimize role conflicts. The greatest potential role conflicts are for the superior. If a system is designed that requires him to act as a judge and a helper at the same time, then we can expect the role of the judge to predominate.

In other words, the superior's efforts to help the subordinate will be canceled out. Thus the superior will lose valuable opportunities to influence performance improvement in the subordinate.

To a great extent, the role the superior plays determines the role the subordinate will play. If the superior comes on strongly as a judge, then there is every reason to believe that the subordinate will come on strongly as a defendant. These two roles tend to create the defensiveness found in so many appraisal sessions, causing great discomfort to both the superior and the subordinate. These sessions also tend not to be very productive in terms of improved performance and superior-subordinate relationships.

In situations where the superior casts himself in the role of helper, the subordinate is more openly willing to deal with his performance deficiencies in a more constructive manner.[8] In this type of environment, performance deficiencies are dealt with as problems and constructive solutions are sought.

What all this means is that we have to make clear in our minds what the objective of goal setting and performance review is. We need to identify the methods and establish the appropriate roles for the superior and subordinate. In addition, and perhaps most important, we must design goal-setting and performance-review methods to avoid role conflict for the superior. If we build role conflict into goal-setting and performance-review methods by making them multipurpose, then we are back where we started—we are back to a system that emphasizes judgment, almost insures defensiveness, and cancels out opportunities for constructive efforts for improvement.

And yet there are numerous examples of goal-setting and performance-review systems, under the title of MBO, that are multipurpose. The multipurpose nature of these systems becomes evident in the performance-review sessions. In some systems goals are rated and the superior is called upon to justify each rating. In one system, performance was rated and multiplied by a weighting assigned to a goal. The products thus derived for each goal were summed and used as a basis for determining salary increases.

These procedures appear to be quite rational and logical. However, the problem is that they do not take into account certain facets of human behavior. In particular, they do not take into account what human beings do in threatening situations. In such situations people tend to become

---

[8]E. Kay, ''A Comparison of a Work Planning Program with the Annual Performance Appraisal Interview Approach,'' General Electric Company Behavioral Research Service, 1964.

defensive or to lower their levels of aspiration. The results are uncomfortable and nonproductive review sessions and the establishment of "safe" goals. Goals that involve stretch, risk, or innovation are to be avoided because they involve punishment. This is why some researchers have stressed separation of appraisal methods—with the prime objective of (a) avoiding or minimizing role conflict in the superior with its disruptive and nonproductive effects, and (b) maximizing the superior's constructive helper role.[9]

Goal-setting and performance-review methods have great potential for improved job understanding and improved levels of performance, *providing* they are designed and implemented to give maximum emphasis to the superior's role as a helper. If they have multipurpose objectives, then they typically fail, get watered down, and eventually are abandoned. This is a clear-cut choice.

In practice, it does not seem possible to completely separate the potentially negative effects of the summary appraisal on other performance discussions. For example, the results of the periodic review sessions relative to goals ultimately will become part of the annual salary review. Regardless of how "pure" the periodic review sessions are in terms of their help orientation, our compensation systems are designed to make use of this performance information. Eventually, we may be able to design our compensation systems to eliminate this negative effect, but this does not seem likely at this time. For the present time we should try to minimize the effects of information from a judgmental situation on the help-oriented sessions. This can be done by having more frequent review sessions so that negative information which shows up at a later date will not come as a surprise. More frequent review sessions also help to establish the role of the superior as someone who is genuinely trying to help, thus building his credibility in the judgmental salary review session. In addition, if there is an equitable salary system which is widely communicated, then there is also the support of a creditable compensation system for this session.

BEHAVIORAL CONSIDERATIONS

So far, the discussion has emphasized the separation of appraisal by purpose and the avoidance of building in role conflicts in the superior's use of appraisal methods. We have suggested that goal-setting and

---

[9]E. Kay, H. H. Meyer, and J. R. P. French, Jr., "Effects of Threat in a Performance Appraisal Interview," *Journal of Applied Psychology*, Vol. 49, No. 5 (1965), pp. 311–317

performance-review methods offer a significant opportunity for the superior to emphasize his role as a helper to the subordinate. In the remainder of this chapter, we will describe a goal-setting and performance-review cycle and discuss the behavioral factors that influence the successful use of this method.

The goal-setting and performance-review model used here to illustrate the relevant behavioral factors was developed by Huse and Kay.[10] This model, called "work planning and review," was developed from the research on performance appraisal conducted at General Electric, and itself was the subject of additional research.[11, 12] A flowchart outlining the work planning and review method is shown in Figure 4.

Work planning and review consists of a number of distinct steps:

PRIOR COMMUNICATION

Before any planning activities there should be a communication phase. In this communication phase the superior and subordinate should review the major responsibilities and performance measurements in the subordinate's position to insure that they adequately reflect the job. In addition, the superior should give the subordinate as much information as he can about business needs, about company plans and objectives, about any special problems of the organization, and about budget constraints. It is also of some value for the superior to make the employee aware of his goals and the problems he is facing as well as his budget constraints. The intent of the prior communications, of course, is to provide the subordinate with as broad as possible a business context for his subsequent planning efforts.

GOAL SETTING

The end product of goal setting is a series of statements of what the subordinate will do in some future time period, the relative priority he will attach to his efforts, and how he will be measured. These statements represent the understanding between the superior and subordinate as to what the subordinate will strive to accomplish. Looked at another way, goal setting represents that part of the process with the greatest potential for helping the subordinate understand what is expected of him.

[10]E. Huse and E. Kay, "Improving Employee Productivity Through Work Planning." In Jerome Blood, ed., *The Personnel Job in a Changing World.* AMA Management Report No. 80, 1964.

[11]E. Kay, op. cit., 1964.

[12]E. Kay and R. Hastman, "An Evaluation of Work Planning and Goal Setting Discussions," General Electric Company Behavioral Research Service, 1966.

4. Work planning and review.

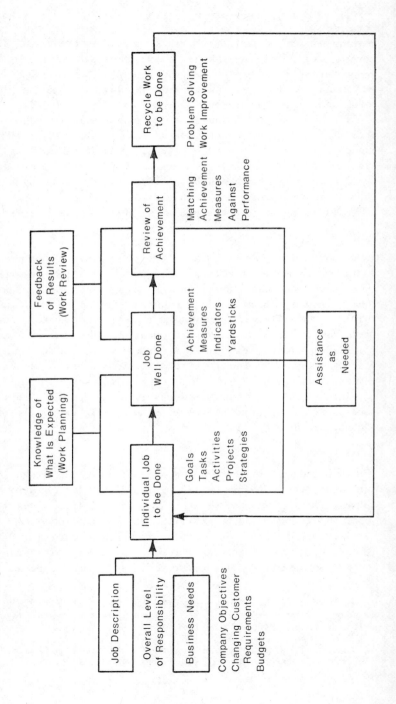

Carroll and Tosi[13] have reported on a study of an MBO program very similar in concept to work planning and review. They found that more difficult goals—clear, important, and relevant goals—and the establishment of priorities for those goals lead the subordinates to feel positive about the program; in some instances there were reports of improved relationships between the subordinates and their superior.

These findings represent an important contribution to our understanding of the behavioral aspects of the goal-setting process. Most of the positive findings relate characteristics of the goals—difficulty, clarity, importance, priorities—which help the subordinate to better understand what is expected of him and give importance to what is expected of him. In other words, subordinates are positive toward the program when it helps them to clarify and gain agreement on what is expected of them.

Interestingly, Carroll and Tosi also found that the amount of influence subordinates had on the goals was not related to their acceptance of the program. In other words, the superior need not change his style of managing with subordinates in goal-setting sessions. A change in the superior's style, that is, allowing the subordinates more or less influence than usual, could have negative effects. The negative effects were evidenced in a decrease in performance when the usual level of participation was either increased or decreased in the goal-setting session.

High-quality goals. We can reasonably conclude that superiors should concentrate on the quality of the goals in the goal-setting session while maintaining their usual relationship with the subordinates. Here are some guidelines for setting better quality goals:

1. A goal implies some achievement as a result of the subordinate doing something. The initial step in clarifying a goal is to begin with "to," followed by a verb: to reduce, to provide, to identify.

2. Each goal should relate to a single *end result.* This pinpoints what is expected and also permits more specific measurement—for example, "To reduce turnover by 10 percent by the end of the fourth quarter." The end result, in this case, is the reduction of turnover. This goal can be further clarified by specifying the area(s) where turnover will be reduced: "To reduce turnover in Area B-7 by 10 percent by the end of the fourth quarter."

3. The measurement should be stated in quantitative terms insofar as is possible. For turnover reduction the quantitative measurement is a 10 percent reduction. This, of course, implies the availability of turnover data for an agreed-upon base period against which the measurement will be taken.

[13]J. C. Carroll and H. L. Tosi, Jr., *Management by Objectives: Applications and Research.* New York: Macmillan, 1973.

Some goals are difficult to specify quantitatively—for example, "To improve the quality of field service manuals." The key question is, "What is a better quality manual?" Is it more readable, shorter, longer, contain more or less illustrations? What is meant by better quality is something that the superior and subordinate should discuss and specify in as much detail as possible in *advance* of the work being done. In such situations the superior might provide sample material as an example of high-quality features.

4. The goal should specify when the end result will be achieved. In the above example, the end result will be met by the end of the fourth quarter. This helps the subordinate to lay out the steps he has to take to meet the due date. It enables the superior and subordinate to measure progress in reaching the end result and signals a review of the total goal.

Level of difficulty. Setting the level of difficulty of goals is a much subtler process. There is a fine but very subjective line between a goal that is regarded as difficult and achievable and a goal that is regarded as difficult and impossible to achieve. Stedry and Kay's[14] findings would seem to prove that there isn't any difference between the two kinds of goals. For example, they found that production foremen who perceived goals as difficult but not impossible to achieve showed significant decreases in performance. There is no hard-and-fast rule for setting the level of difficulty for a goal, but the superior should be sensitive to pushing the level of difficulty into the impossible-to-achieve range.

From time to time the superior may have subordinates who tend to set either very low goals or very high but unrealistic goals. The individual who sets very low goals, of course, is playing it safe. He will not achieve much but he is certain to achieve what he said he would. Such people usually are concerned with the consequences of failure. My experience has shown that their achievement levels can be raised in small increments, but that the superior must be supportive. As the subordinate experiences small increments of achievement, he becomes more confident and is willing to assume more risks.

The person who establishes unrealistically high goals also is concerned with the consequences of failure. By setting very high goals, he gives the impression of trying. When he fails to reach his goals, he has a built-in excuse for failure. He can at least say that he tried. Attempts by superiors to have such people reduce their goals to more realistic levels usually are not successful. They tend to resist realistic goals

[14]A. C. Stedry and E. Kay, "The Effects of Goal Difficulty on Performance: A Field Experiment," *Behavioral Science,* Vol. 11 (1966), pp. 459–470.

because they then lose the excuse for failure. My experience has shown that these people tend to voluntarily terminate or seek a transfer when pressured to reduce their goals to realistic levels. Of course, if by happenstance such a person should achieve one of his unrealistic goals, then he becomes impossible to live with!

Priorities. The establishment of priorities also requires careful analysis by the superior and subordinate. Mali suggests that goals be ranked according to potential payoff and that only those with the highest payoff be worked on. There are clear-cut situations where the elaborate payoff analysis that he suggests can be useful. Priorities, however, are not always clearly related to potential payoff. Quite frequently the middle manager is part of a larger chain of events, and it is not clear to him from where he sits as to where he should allocate his greatest efforts. The superior can be of great value here by providing the "big picture."

PERFORMANCE REVIEW

Performance review involves an important behavioral process that is referred to as feedback or knowledge of results. Some values of receiving feedback are obvious. The individual who has set a goal and receives feedback about where he stands relative to the achievement of the goal is in the possession of very useful information. Not only does he get some measure of satisfaction or dissatisfaction from the feedback but it also guides or adjusts his behavior in respect to the goal. If the feedback indicates that he is not making the progress he should, he has a signal to intensify his efforts or to examine and adjust his efforts or methods toward achieving the goal.

Of course, there are other things he can do. He can abandon the goal if it appears that he cannot achieve it, or he can lower the goal to make it more achievable. He also can set higher levels of achievement for himself when he is satisfied that he can achieve his current goals.

The results of the GE study of performance appraisals indicated that too great an emphasis on criticism resulted in high defensiveness and subsequent lack of performance improvement by subordinates. Positive feedback had no effect on performance. It appeared in this study that praise was being used as part of the "sandwich technique" described by Maier, evidenced by the fact that subordinates who received large amounts of criticism in their appraisals also received large amounts of praise. This study suggests that the manner in which the feedback is given affects the way it is received and used by subordinates.

In their study of an MBO system, Carroll and Tosi report additional finds on the nature and effects of feedback:

1. More frequent reviews resulted in higher satisfaction with the program, higher goal achievement, and improved relations with the superior compared to previous time periods.
2. Higher amounts of praise and lower amounts of criticism resulted in higher reported goal achievement and higher levels of achievement being set for the next time period.
3. Subordinate perceptions that the superior was interested in goal achievement where related to more positive feelings about the program.

Their findings tend to confirm the GE results and extend our knowledge of the review process. The two studies show that the characteristics of an effective review session include

- A superior who is interested in the program and who expects results
- An emphasis on positive results rather than negative results
- More frequent review sessions

One might raise the question here as to how to deal with a situation where the subordinate's performance is more negative than positive. Of course, one could resort to the sandwich technique, but this would require the superior to indulge in fabricated positive platitudes which tend to be quite transparent. Bassett and Meyer[15] found self-appraisal a useful means for dealing with negative aspects of performance. Subordinates who prepared their own appraisals were less defensive in discussing poor performance than those who had received manager-initiated appraisals. This suggests the use of subordinate-initiated performance reviews, particularly in situations where there are many negatives to deal with.

Carroll and Tosi do not specify the number of reviews or feedback sessions conducted. Thus from their data we cannot derive a specific number as a guideline. In general, we would discourage the search for a magic number and encourage the use of judgment in specific situations. In Kay and Hastman's study the frequency of review sessions varied considerably, for what appeared to be good reasons. More frequent sessions (six to eight a year) were conducted with poorer performing subordinates and relatively new employees. Less frequent sessions (one to three a year) were conducted with more experienced subordinates and those in whom the superior had a great deal of confidence.

Situational factors also tend to affect the number of review sessions.

[15]G. A. Bassett and H. H. Meyer, "Performance Appraisal Based on Self-Review," *Personnel Psychology*, Vol. 21 (1968), pp. 421–430.

If business conditions change, as they often do, then a review is necessary to reestablish priorities. Managers tend to develop a good feel for the need for reviews as a result of subordinate or situational factors and should be encouraged to use their judgment and to be flexible. The worst possible situation is where goals are established on the first day of the fiscal year and not reviewed until the last day with no intervening reviews. This approach presupposes that nothing changes in the course of the year and that there are no subordinate needs that would be satisfied by feedback.

RECYCLE WORK TO BE DONE

This phase of the goal-setting and performance-review process is suggestive of the fact that the process is cyclical and continuous. Goal setting leads to performance reviews and performance reviews lead to an updating of goals, measurements, and priorities which in turn lead to additional reviews. In this way goal setting and performance review become part of the total management process.

It should be fairly obvious by now that goal-setting and performance-review activities offer significant opportunities for one-on-one dialogs between top managers and middle managers. These methods offer significant opportunities to increase the mutual understanding of what is expected from the middle manager, to plan for the middle manager's development, and to provide a constructive motivational climate for performance improvement. One of the major objections to goal-setting and performance-review methods is that it takes time. If we assume that the goal-setting and performance-review process is no more complicated than the situation calls for, then I see the time allocation problem as a matter of priorities and value received for the time spent doing it. We seem to have the time to clear up the problems resulting from poor mutual understanding relative to job expectations. How much time is it worth to reduce the number and severity of such misunderstandings and to provide a more constructive motivational climate to boot?

chapter eight

Places to Go and to Grow:
New Alternatives
for Middle Managers

THE BOXING-IN PHENOMENON is the single greatest factor that adversely affects the behavior of middle managers. The phenomenon arises from the pyramidal nature of organization structures: As a person moves up the hierarchy, opportunities for subsequent upward moves are diminished significantly and at some point he plateaus out. Also, opportunities for lateral movement diminish because the individual lacks experience in other functions to which he might be moved, and his salary is too high to move him to an area where he will be regarded as a beginner.

The boxing-in phenomenon represents a complex set of individual and situational factors. The usual approach to dealing with its reactions is to try to do something to or with the individual in order to make *him* more responsive to the situation. Thus it is not uncommon for top management to opt for training approaches or motivational gimmicks in order to stimulate middle managers. At best, the effects of these approaches are short-lived because, in the total equation that represents behavior, it is also necessary to consider and *change* those aspects of the situation that have adverse effects on the middle manager's behavior.

$$\text{Behavior} = f \text{ (Person} \times \text{Environment)}$$

This equation shows two important considerations. The first is that behavior results from characteristics of both the person and the environment. The second is that behavior is a *multiplicative* function of the two factors. If one is zero or close to zero, then the desired or expected behavior will not be forthcoming. For example, a person with little or no aptitudes for a job could not be expected to perform adequately in the most ideal environment. Conversely, a person with the highest of abilities and aptitudes could not be expected to perform adequately in a poor environment.

In this chapter we will address ourselves primarily to changes that can be made in certain aspects of the middle manager's work environment. We stress changes in the environment rather than in the middle managers themselves in order to redress the imbalance caused by the current over-emphasis on changing the person and because there are significant opportunities to improve the middle manager environment.

The basic approach is to provide opportunities within the work environment that will allow continued psychological growth, increased contributions to the organization, and continuing opportunities for increased rewards without the necessity of being promoted to a higher level in the hierarchy. Many of the alternatives that will be considered can take place within the individual's current organization; he need not change jobs to achieve an improved environment. We will also consider alternatives where it is best for a person to leave his organization and seek another environment.

ALTERNATIVES WITHIN THE ORGANIZATION

JOB ROTATION

One approach to providing middle managers with continued opportunities for growth is to rotate them laterally through positions in other functions. For reasons already cited (the relatively high salaries and so on) this is not usually done. In spite of these disadvantages, however, a number of organizations have initiated formal rotation programs or have instituted policies that sanction and encourage such rotation.

The characteristics of the rotation programs are as follows:

Rotation is voluntary and selective. The program is available to middle managers who want it, but not all are selected. Considerable professional counseling is done with the individual who opts for this approach in terms of his objectives, what the change will require of him, and the risks involved.

Rotation is lateral in terms of salary and organization levels. The employee who rotates does so at his current salary and organization levels. There are no demotions and pay cuts involved. Thus his current status is preserved. There is a clear recognition by the top management that the individual probably is overpaid somewhat for his contribution for a certain time period. There is also a clear recognition, however, that the overpayment is a direct investment in maintaining continued motivation and expanding the skills of a key manpower source. This realization is an important one and is the basis for the entire approach.

The middle manager is protected in the event of failure. One of the issues that arises in rotation programs is how to handle failure on the assignment to which the individual is rotated. How is the individual to be judged? On his past achievements? On the assignment to which he rotated? Or both?

Basically, the philosophy that has evolved is to measure the individual on his past achievements, to remove him from the rotational assignment on which he may be failing, and to attempt to reposition him where he has already demonstrated success. The intent here is to avoid, as much as possible, the stigma usually associated with failure which could force the individual to leave or to be buried in some obscure or harmless position.

In one rotation program, which has been in operation for approximately seven years, there have been two cases out of approximately 20 where the middle managers have had to be taken off a rotation assignment and reassigned. In both instances the individuals were able to go back to their previous functional areas, not necessarily their previous jobs, and readjust comfortably.

Successful rotation can lead to additional rotation. In the rotation program just cited, several people are now rotating into their second round of assignments in new functional areas. Others have stayed in their new functional areas and could reasonably be expected to take on additional assignments in the new functions. The remainder have gone back to their original functional areas—some to their original positions and some to other positions in their original function.

As can be seen, a relatively simple rotation program can result in a great deal of lateral movement in a short period of time. The benefits that have been cited by top management and middle management of such a program are these:

● It stimulates the middle manager who might otherwise get turned off or leave.

● Obviously, it provides the rotated manager with a broader set of skills but it also gives him a broader and more realistic perspective of how the business operates. A middle manager who performs a job in a different function not only learns the necessary new skills but he also experiences the problems inherent in the new function. In particular, he gets some firsthand insights into the problems that he, in his old function, has caused in his new area. If he should return to his old function, he is in a much better position to work better with the other function. The insights gained in cross-functional relation assignments are very similar to those gained in the team-building sessions described in Chapter 7.

• It provides visible evidence that the organization is aware of middle manager needs and is doing something constructive.

JOB ENRICHMENT

Job enrichment is usually discussed in relation to clerical or blue collar positions. However, it is also relevant to the middle management ranks. Job enrichment methods are based on a theory of motivation developed by Herzberg and associates.[1] The theory postulates two sets of motivational influences that must be satisfied to achieve maximum job performance:

Demotivators. Demotivators are elements in the work environment that can *decrease* motivation: pay, benefits, security, supervision, and working conditions. If a work environment is neutral or positive in respect to these factors, then the most that can be hoped for is that the employee's motivation will not decrease. He will not be particularly positive as a result; he will just not be negative. Concern about the demotivators, or hygiene factors, as they are also called, is needed to prevent a decrease in motivation.

Motivators. Motivators are the characteristics of the work or job itself. If the job provides responsibility, growth, and opportunity for achievement and recognition, then these job characteristics in themselves will provide a high degree of intrinsic motivation.

Techniques for Job Enrichment

This two-factor theory led to the use of job enrichment as a way of increasing the motivational potential of the job itself—calling for the building of more motivators into the job. There are three basic techniques of enriching jobs by building in motivational elements:

Eliminating unmotivating tasks. This method consists of examining the content of a job and eliminating those factors that are low in respect to responsibility, growth, and achievement. Just their elimination leaves an enriched job in terms of the remaining tasks.

Horizontal stretching. Horizontal expansion is achieved by adding

[1]Frederick Herzberg, *Work and the Nature of Man.* Cleveland: World Publishing, 1966.

elements from other jobs, which, in effect, provide a greater variety and perhaps increased complexity. In the clerical and blue collar ranks sometimes the job is stretched horizontally by giving the individual or team the responsibility for a complete, identifiable end product. The important thing in horizontal stretching is that the added tasks be motivating—representing genuine increments in growth, responsibility, and achievement.

Vertical loading. This method consists of adding tasks to a job that previously had been done at higher levels in the organization. In addition to specific tasks, vertical loading may include increased participation in the decision-making process and increased authority.

Job enrichment methods have not been extensively applied to middle management positions, but examples of their use can be cited here.

Horizontal Stretching

In a development laboratory the work was organized by technical or scientific disciplines. In addition to doing development work on applications, the laboratory also became extensively involved in the analysis of product problems in the field. In group sessions, the middle managers in the laboratory expressed general feelings of dissatisfaction with their jobs. When pressed for specifics, they indicated that while they were responsible for the activities of their specific disciplines, they did not feel any great responsibility for measurable or significant results. This feeling was explored in more depth; it seemed to result from the fact that very seldom were they held responsible for a total problem. For example, when a problem with a product arose in the field, the marketing people would come to the laboratory for help. In the laboratory, the problem was reviewed by a high-level committee, assigned a priority, and parceled out to various technical specialties for analysis. Thus the middle manager was given a problem in which his particular specialty had an opportunity to see the entire problem or to deal with it in a total sense. At times, this lack of identity with the problem proved to be an embarrassment to the laboratory as it was difficult for the field people to find anyone in the laboratory who could talk knowledgeably about the *total* problem for which they were seeking help.

The horizontal job enrichment done in this situation gave a middle manager complete responsibility for a particular problem. Typically, the middle manager was given a problem in which his particular specialty would contribute the most to the analysis. In addition, the manager was expected to call upon the services of his colleagues for the analysis. The manager was expected to come up with a complete analysis and set of recommendations and to "speak for" the laboratory to the organiza-tion that referred the problem. In essence, the horizontal enrichment stretched the job from that of managing a technical specialty to that of managing the entire solution of a problem.

This enrichment had several interesting results. First, it greatly increased the actual and felt responsibilities of the middle managers as it gave them a total result to achieve and a client interface. Second, it resulted in the enrichment for other jobs that the manager supervised. The need for coordination and planning between technical groups increased, which was subsequently delegated to project leaders and senior technical specialists. These people now also shared in some of the increased responsibility for pulling together the results for a total problem rather than just the part relating to their own specialty.

Vertical Loading

A group of middle managers in a manufacturing organization had had several team-building sessions with top management. Job enrichment of the middle manager's job had come up from time to time as a topic, and the group decided to deal with this subject in a more specific way. In particular, they decided to look at opportunities for vertical loading, that is, opportunities to enrich the middle manager positions by incor-porating meaningful activities performed at a higher organization level. The higher-level position they looked at for more meaningful activities was that of the manufacturing manager, their superior, and the examina-tion resulted in the following:

1. *Rejection of trivia.* The middle managers rejected the delegation of trivia from the manufacturing manager to them in the name of job enrichment. If the manufacturing manager was experiencing too much trivia in his job, then he would have to find a different way to deal with it.

2. *Clarification and delegation of approval authorities.* The middle managers strongly felt that clarification and specific delegation of approval authorities would help to make their jobs more meaningful. Actually, what they were saying was that the uncertainty about and lack of approval authorities resulted in a sense of "incompleteness" about their jobs. In other words, they could go so far with a situation, at which point they had to get confirmation from the manufacturing manager for the course of action they felt to be appropriate. As one manager put it, "We always have to get permission to do the obvious."

The managers dealt with the matter of delegation and clarification of approval authority by a method they dubbed the decision-making inventory (DMI). Basically, their approach consisted of listing generic categories of decisions—for example, master schedule, operating budgets, method changes, salary increases—in which they were involved. They used a format similar to that in Table 5 and coded each decision category according to who decided, who made input to the decision, and who needed to be informed about the decision. They then agreed upon changes in the locus of decision making with an emphasis on pushing more decision-making responsibility down to the middle managers.

Table 5 shows the results of their deliberations for four decision categories. In the case of operating budgets, the manufacturing manager made the decision based on inputs from the middle managers. He also kept them informed about his decision. For this decision category, they decided that there would be no change in the future; the manufacturing manager would continue to make the final decision for the overall budgets. They did decide, however, that the middle managers would have more control over the day-to-day decisions affecting operating budgets. Thus

Table 5. Decision-making inventory.

Decision Category	Mfg. Mgr.	Prod. Mgr. A	Prod. Mgr. B	Prod. Mgr. C	Mfg. Engr.	Prod. Control	Materials Mgr.
Operating budgets							
Now	1	2, 3	2, 3	2, 3	2, 3	2, 3	2, 3
Future	1	2, 3	2, 3	2, 3	2, 3	2, 3	2, 3
Day-to-day decisions affecting operating budgets							
Now	1	2, 3	2, 3	2, 3	2, 3	2, 3	2, 3
Future	2, 3	1, 2	1, 2	1, 2	1, 2	1, 2	1, 2
Method changes							
Now	1	2, 3	2, 3	2, 3	2, 3	3	3
Future	2, 3	2, 3	2, 3	2, 3	1, 2	3	3
Overtime approval							
Now	1	2, 3	2, 3	2, 3	2, 3	2, 3	2, 3
Future	3	1, 2	1, 2	1, 2	1, 2	1, 2	1, 2

CODE: 1—Who decides.
2—Who makes input to the decision.
3—Who needs to be informed about the decision.

if a middle manager had to reallocate resources to meet a particular situation, he could do so without seeking the approval of his superior. He need only inform him of the decision. This gave the middle managers greater flexibility. The only constraint was that he could not exceed his total operating budget.

In the area of method changes, the decision making shifted from the manufacturing manager to the manufacturing engineering manager. The role of the other middle managers was not affected. For overtime approval, the decision making shifted from the manufacturing manager to each of the middle managers.

Actually, what emerged from this effort was a pattern in which the manufacturing manager made the decisions in "big picture" areas (master schedules, operating budgets), with the middle managers getting more autonomy and flexibility in dealing with day-to-day matters.

3. *Increased departmentwide responsibilities.* The group also examined ways that would enable the middle managers to perform their jobs with the perspective of the manufacturing manager, that is, with the point of view of the total manufacturing department in mind. Each middle manager was given an opportunity to play a lead role in an activity that cut across the entire department. In the lead role the middle manager acted as if he were the manufacturing manager and provided the necessary leadership to achieve a departmentwide result. The middle managers assumed lead roles for such varied activities as cost reduction programs, reduction of absenteeism, and the introduction of a new product line.

TASK FORCES, PROJECT TEAMS, TEMPORARY STAFF ASSIGNMENTS

Job rotation and job enrichment are alternatives that may result in long-term or permanent solutions to the boxing-in problem. When these approaches cannot be used, it may be necessary and desirable to turn to more temporary solutions, such as task forces, project teams, and temporary staff assignments, to offer the manager some relief from the boxing-in effects. From time to time, organizations need ad hoc groups to deal with special situations. Temporary assignment to a special group can be an important experience to the middle manager, providing the task is a meaningful one.

The value of a temporary group project can best be illustrated with an example. In one large consumer product organization, a number of middle managers are invited to take a temporary assignment (12 to 18 months) on the corporate staff. They convene as a group and are given a specific problem on which to work. The problem typically is one which has great significance to the organization. The group is charged with coming up with a solution, recommendations, and an implementation plan for dealing with the problem. They are told that their recommendations will be followed unless they come up with something which is way off base. The latter point is an important element in the assignment. The group is told that they have an opportunity to solve a significant problem or to create a significant change and that they will not be second-guessed or just writing a report on which someone else will act. Thus top management is putting faith in the middle management and offering them a significant challenge.

One of the temporary staff groups in this organization developed and implemented a new compensation system for the organization. They started out feeling somewhat overwhelmed by the assignment because of the potential impact of what they were asked to do and because they did not feel they had any particular expertise in this area. They evaluated and selected a compensation consultant to help them, and very quickly found themselves involved in all the technical as well as psychological aspects of compensation. Their efforts took them into every corner of the organization. At the end of their study they made a presentation to the top executives who accepted their recommendations. The effect of this type of experience on the group members was nothing short of profound. They had learned a great deal and had an opportunity to become involved in a corporatewide activity. In addition, they were justifiably proud of their results. Almost all the members of this group went back to their original assignments. Several were transferred or promoted. Although most went back to the same old box on the organization chart, the temporary experience was a significant motivational lift.

This example illustrates some of the important characteristics of a temporary assignment. First, they were asked to deal with a significant problem. Second, they were given almost complete responsibility for dealing with it. And third, they could expect to see the results of their efforts used. These conditions produced a highly motivating climate, a high commitment to dealing with the problem and to the group, and a great deal of individual learning. Temporary assignments that do not approach these criteria are meaningless to those involved.

ALTERNATIVES OUTSIDE THE ORGANIZATION

Realistically, we should not expect all middle managers to want to stay with their organization through their total career. There is some evidence that considerable numbers of people would leave in midcareer for other pursuits. For example, in *The Changing Success Ethic*[2] 55 percent of the surveyed middle managers indicated that they had changed or considered changing their occupational field during the last five years. Forty-four percent indicated that there was an occupational field in which they would rather be than their present line of work; of these, approximately three-fourths expected to be searching for a way to make a career change in the foreseeable future. If we extrapolate from these numbers, 25 to 30 percent of the middle managers surveyed expected to be searching for a way to make a career change in the foreseeable future.

Entine, who conducted the New Careers Program at Columbia University from 1963 to 1969, reported that 4,000 inquiries were received during the first two years of the program and approximately 75 to 100 inquiries per month for the next three years.[3] Originally, this program was designed to help people between the ages of 45 and 55 who held positions of responsibility in business to make career shifts into the not-for-profit service sectors, such as educational, social work, and other service organizations. One significant thing in this program was this sustained high volume of inquiries. The inquiries not only came from persons who fit the criteria for the program but from others from a wide variety of occupations and walks of life.

These data suggest a pent-up demand for second careers on all levels of the workforce. At this point, it is not possible to make any meaningful estimate of the numbers of people who would or should make such a change either in their own organization or outside of it. However, it does appear that there is enough of a need to consider the ways of making external alternatives, that is, leaving the organization, more viable.

A frequently mentioned external alternative is a second career. Second careers are usually regarded as an external alternative because these opportunities generally are not available within an individual's organization for reasons already cited. Motivation for a second career may come from many sources. A desire to use a broader set of skills, changing interests, and a desire to embark in new fields that have developed since initial graduation from college are just a few. Second careers have not been precisely defined, but they seem to offer the following possibilities:

[2]Dale Tarnowieski, AMA Research Report, 1973.
[3]Alan Entine, "Second Careers, Experience and Expectations." In H. L. Sheppard and Neal Q. Herrick, eds., *Where Have All the Robots Gone?* New York: Free Press, 1970.

- Self-employment or small-scale businesses
- A completely new kind of work requiring a new set of knowledge and skills
- The use of existing skills but in a radically different environment

SELF-EMPLOYMENT OR SMALL-SCALE BUSINESSES

This alternative, which is becoming increasingly rarer in the United States (only approximately 6 to 7 percent of the total workforce) is a choice for those who have entrepreneurial motivations that cannot be satisfied within their organizations. Self-employment offers the opportunity to engage in all the business functions, perhaps to nurture a business so that he can hire other people. Self-employment and small-scale businesses are vulnerable economically but do provide independence and possible significant financial gains.

The cases that I have been following of middle managers who have moved to self-employment or a small-scale business appear to have one important characteristic in common: the individual transitioned to self-employment or a small-scale business over a period of years. In other words, the first career and new career overlapped by approximately three to five years. The new career activity was developed on a part-time basis until it was financially viable or until circumstances such as a loss of job forced him into it full-time. In several cases the second career was planned with the deliberate purpose of transitioning; in other cases it was something the individual got into by chance or through some special interest he had. In any event, the paralleling emerges as a significant factor. It would appear that it provides a relatively low-risk way of getting started.

COMPLETELY NEW KIND OF WORK

In all probability a completely new kind of work requiring a new set of knowledge and skills will require some education. The education to support a new career might be obtained in parallel with the first career by taking courses at night, or one can go to school full-time if financially feasible. The pros and cons of each approach are fairly obvious. Night courses take longer but the individual is able to maintain his source of income in the process. He may also have opportunities for tuition refunds from his employer for some of the courses. Full-time attendance at school, of course, shortens the time spent in obtaining the necessary education and may provide a better educational climate. However, there is then the problem of how to finance this time period.

Some universities have programs designed for adult students that enable them to continue working and to achieve their education through mostly independent study and minimal on-campus residence. The Liberal Studies Program at the University of Oklahoma is one such example. Perhaps the best way to describe the program is to quote from a letter sent to me by one of the first persons to enroll in the Bachelor of Liberal Studies Program at this university. He describes his undergraduate work in this program as follows:

> When I finally got around to completing my degree, I took it through independent study at the University of Oklahoma. I don't know whether you've heard about the BLS [Bachelor of Liberal Studies] program or not, but it has an interesting history.
>
> It was begun in 1961 under a Kellogg Foundation grant of $100,000. It works like this: Students are enrolled at the campus or by mail; they can reside anywhere in the world. After initial testing to determine approximate educational level, the student is assigned a faculty adviser on the doctorate level (usually). The faculty adviser and the student then design a series of in-depth readings, after the student has chosen his initial "area" of work.
>
> There are three areas, each of a year's duration: the social sciences, the natural sciences, the humanities, and a fourth "inter-area" that combines the prior three. The inter-area involves an in-depth study or paper on an appropriate theme selected by the student and approved by the adviser.
>
> There are no lessons flying back and forth; the student reads, studies, tests his emerging understanding in life, and when he is ready, completes a comprehensive exam in the area in which he's working. If he passes, he's eligible to spend three weeks in residence on the campus in a special seminar with up to 25 other people who have been studying in the same area. The seminars are—and were for me—the most exciting, profound learning experiences I've encountered anywhere. OU faculty people fight to teach the seminars—because the students are a real challenge. Any one group may be composed of managers, engineers, physicians, housewives, military personnel, church men, retired people, hourly workers: you name it—a real cross section.
>
> So far, the program has graduated about 350 people. About 70 percent have gone on into graduate work in just about every discipline you can name, from law to philosophy, and everything in between. There are about 2,200 people enrolled now; all graduates have taken the GRE and only one has scored under the national average. Most score well above, and one even exceeded the best national score.
>
> Aside from the basic degree program, students who wish to obtain a masters through independent study may qualify for work in the

MLS program. There is also a junior college option, whereby a person with the basic two years can spend two additional years in the BLS program and come out with the degree. This is not a diploma mill; it is a program designed for self-starters. I have seen profound changes and great growth in people who were with me in the earliest years of the program. I began in 1962 and finished in 1966, when I was 40 years old.

The letter says quite a bit about what can be achieved through new models of adult education. It departs sharply from the typical campus residence, classroom instruction, and grading. Although the program does not have a strong vocation orientation, it offers flexibility and opportunities for the mature, motivated adult who is pursuing an education as a basis for a significant change in his life.

The person considering a career change to a different kind of work would also benefit from counseling in respect to employment opportunities in the new field, job requirements, and some assurance about the ability to meet the educational requirements. In Entine's program, counseling was provided through monthly group meetings in which the participants shared common experiences and heard presentations about existing opportunities in their fields of interest. In addition, individual counseling was provided as needed on personal and academic problems.

PERSONNEL POLICIES AND PRACTICES
TO SUPPORT NEW ALTERNATIVES

For new alternatives to be viable, support with appropriate policies and practices is necessary. Current personnel practices will have to be modified or new policies created to achieve the desired effects. Perhaps the greatest changes we can anticipate in personnel policies to support new alternatives are provision for more flexibility and matching policies to human development needs as opposed to relatively inflexible policies designed primarily to serve organizational needs.

Many personnel practices tend to take on a logic and a life of their own and in time become institutionalized. The logic, generally, is an organizational need, for example, a need for a continuous flow of high potential candidates or an equitable compensation system. Each perceived personnel need is then embodied in a procedure which over time becomes the accepted way of doing things. A personnel system such as compensation is highly institutionalized and supported by a specific technology and, in most organizations, a veil of secrecy. This kind of system becomes inviolate and quite frequently the guardian of the system, the compensation manager, will go to great lengths to defend and preserve it. The system emerges as a fixed quantity, and it is up to individuals to live with it—whether or not it serves their needs. At best a system that is not responsive to human needs is just that—a system without meaning or value to people. At worst, it is a breeding ground for cynicism, frustration, and deception. What we are saying is that if we accept the notion of new alternatives for middle managers as a means of making their work environment more livable, then we must accept the notion of more flexible policies and policies that are more responsive to human needs.

Earlier in this chapter we suggested some new alternatives for middle managers. Now let us take a look at some of the personnel policy changes or innovations that will be needed to support these alternatives.

JOB ROTATION

Some of the specific policy elements that would support job rotation for middle managers are:

Fixed tenure in a job or in a function. A policy that automatically qualifies a middle manager as a candidate for rotation after he has been in a position for a specified number of years would help to focus on those who might benefit from a rotational move. Not every person who is flagged by such a method necessarily would be rotated, but the process would draw attention to him as well as provide a pool from which to select managers for rotation.

Criteria for selecting managers to be rotated. Ideally, the managers to be rotated are those who would benefit the most from such rotation. The problem is that most organizations do not have enough experience in selecting people for such moves. Until such experience accumulates, selection should be of those individuals who best meet the intent of the rotation through desire and ability to learn, willingness to risk a change, evidence that they have mastered their current jobs, low probability of promotion.

The criteria need to be explicit enough so there is little doubt about who should be rotated, and the actions should be reviewed at the higher levels of the organization to ensure that the right people are rotated.

Compensation. What is an equitable way to compensate someone who would be overpaid while he is gaining knowledge and experience in a new functional area? The best answer is not to overpay him or, at a minimum, not to overpay him any more than is necessary. The answer to the question implies two possible courses of action regarding compensation. The first is to cut the person's salary with the understanding that it will be increased as he learns and demonstrates competence in the new area. The second is to hold his salary at its current level and delay additional increases until such time that he starts to meet the requirements of the new job.

Pay cuts, which most managers find difficult to administer, probably is not the way to do it. A freeze on the current salary until the requirements of the new position are met seems to be the better route. In this context goal-setting sessions, which help the rotated person understand what is expected of him in his new position and what he has to achieve to get back on the salary curve, are called for.

Job security. A manager who fails in an assignment to which he is rotated should not lose his previous position with the organization as a result of the failure. He should have the opportunity to move back when a suitable opening occurs. The point is that the organization should not lose a person who has already demonstrated his competence in at least one particular area.

This again points up the importance of selecting the right individual for rotation. Such a person should be acceptable in his back home function. If he is not, then the wrong person was selected for the wrong reasons.

JOB ENRICHMENT

Job enrichment involves adding additional tasks and responsibilities to the manager's job. The intent is to make the job intrinsically more motivating. One aspect of job enrichment to be sensitive to is that it is possible to enrich the job to the point of "bad hygiene." It is possible to add duties and responsibilities to the point where the person feels he is being put upon and underpaid. At this point, he is apt to become demotivated as a result of a perceived inequitable pay situation.

Thus, as jobs are enriched, attention must be paid to the value of the job in terms of the organization's job evaluation. If application of job-evaluation weights to the enriched job shows that it has increased in value, then the job grade should be increased and the incumbent's salary increased, under the applicable rules of the compensation system, if he falls below the position rate for the new job grade.[4] If the job grade is not raised at an appropriate point, then it is reasonable to expect that managers will view "job enrichment" negatively.

Job enrichment will require greater flexibility in the compensation system. It will have to deal with middle manager positions that are more

---

[4]In some compensation systems, the individual's salary can remain below the position rate for certain reasons but for no more than a set period of time.

custom-designed to the needs of the incumbent than is normally done. In addition, job enrichment may result in middle manager positions being evaluated across a greater number of job grades than is now the case. Conceivably, this could create some feelings of inequity in top management as middle manager pay grades get closer to theirs. Some compensation specialists argue that managers will use job enrichment as a guise to give pay increases to middle managers where they might not otherwise be able to. This undoubtedly will be attempted, but it is no different from other attempts to increase the point value of a job through the inclusion of "additional" duties or by giving greater emphasis to certain responsibilities.

For job enrichment to be successful, the personnel policy will have to reflect an understanding of the need for more flexibility in job evaluation and compensation. This will require the compensation administrator to look at middle manager jobs on a more individual basis and to be prepared to evaluate and accept proposed elements for enrichment.

TEMPORARY ASSIGNMENTS

Temporary assignments do not pose any great difficulties or new requirements for personnel practices and policies. It is more a matter of deciding whether such an approach is feasible and of value in organizations. There are two personnel policy and practice areas involved in temporary assignments that should be mentioned.

Compensation and perquisites. Occasionally, individuals who are put on temporary assignments are paid under special compensation programs and have perquisites unique to their regular jobs. For example, a field sales manager, asked to take a temporary task force assignment, may be receiving a significant portion of his compensation from a bonus pool for his division and be entitled to a company car. Should these compensation arrangements and perquisites continue on the temporary assignment, particularly if the temporary assignment may last a year or longer?

The general solution to these types of situations is to treat him as a middle manager in headquarters for the time he is on the temporary assignment. Thus he may have to give up his automobile, and a fixed salary is negotiated with him for the term of the assignment. If there is a bonus or incentive program for middle managers in headquarters, he then becomes eligible to participate in it. These situations arise infrequently but they do require consideration and sensitivity.

The back home job. Most of the managers on temporary assignments should anticipate returning to their back home assignments. Unless the manager is to be promoted or transferred, his position should be preserved for him. This can be done by appointing someone to replace him on an acting basis, thus making clear to everyone that the assignment is temporary. A side benefit is that this is a good opportunity to try out a person in this acting role who is seen as having managerial potential. If he does not measure up, there is no stigma when he leaves the position, as this was expected to happen in any event.

SECOND CAREERS

Second careers may be pursued within the manager's current organization, particularly if job rotation options are available, or outside the employing organization. In either event, it can be to the advantage of certain individuals to pursue second careers and for the organization to be supportive of such pursuits. Pursuit of a second career may allow additional outlets for satisfaction and growth of the individual not available in the organization and perhaps prevent him from becoming a problem in the organization. The personnel policy elements that are important for a second career program are

Self-selection. Essentially the choice to pursue a second career is a choice to voluntarily sever relationships with the organization at a certain point in time. This decision is very basic to the individual and the choice to do so should be his.

Lead time. The best evidence at this time indicates that a second career must run parallel to the first career for a number of years in order to achieve an effective transition. Three to five years seems to be a reasonable time period. If an individual is to have enough working years left to pursue a meaningful second career, then he should start no later than age 50. This means that at the latest, the option to elect a second career to leave the organization should be made when he is in his mid-40s. This age coincides with the peak of the midcareer crisis; and also would have permitted the individual to make enough of a contribution to his organization to warrant their support in making the transition. In this respect, the organization may want to put a floor on the number of years of service with the organization for eligibility in such a program. Fifteen to twenty years of service is an appropriate range.

Preparation. A person who elects to leave for a second career should be provided with some help during the transition years. One kind of help should be counseling—broad enough to cover both financial and vocational matters pertaining to the second career.

Another element in preparation is time. For those who need education to prepare for a second career, time might be made available through sabbaticals or release time from work to attend classes. Another way of providing time is to "step down" the time the individual must be available to the organization as he approaches his cutoff date. For example, in his next to last year he might only work 75 percent of the time; in his last year he might only work half-time.

Among other things, the new alternatives and supporting policies suggested in this chapter will have the effect of raising visible costs. Deliberate raising of visible costs is always difficult, particularly when the offsetting gains are difficult to measure. The visible versus invisible nature of costs quite frequently becomes a barrier to change. In evaluating whether or not to implement policies that will visibly raise costs, it is important for policy makers at least to consider what the hidden costs might be.

Let us take the case of a middle manager who is paid $20,000 per year exclusive of benefits and overhead charges. If we assume he is 75 percent effective, then the invisible cost to the company is $5,000 per year. If we were to spend $20,000 to prepare him for a second career, for example, four years after he left we would have recouped the investment and prevented any further losses. Of course, the true cost to an organization of an ineffective middle manager is apt to be much more. Keep in mind that the middle manager impacts on his peers as well as on many people below him. How do you put a dollar figure on lack of cooperation with other middle managers, excessive bureaucracy, unresponsiveness to organization goals, and poor implementation with individuals lower in the hierarchy? If these could be measured, then the increased visible costs of the new alternatives would be a bargain.

chapter nine

The Organization of the Future:
What Role for Middle Managers?

THE PRECEDING THREE chapters have dealt with remedial approaches to the current problems of middle managers. We have considered ways to bring about a more optimal distribution of authority within the middle management ranks, new alternatives to deal with the boxing-in problems, and some approaches to hygiene factors. We should anticipate that changes will take place in the middle manager environment whether or not top management makes specific interventions to deal with current problems. In this chapter we will look at some of the changes that are occurring or are on the horizon in organizations and how they might affect the middle manager.

The three future-oriented aspects of the organization that we will examine in this chapter are (1) the effect of information technology on the middle managers, (2) the effect of the application of behavioral science technology in other parts of the organization on the middle managers, and (3) the innovations in the use of organization structure. Of the three, computer technology and applications are by far the most advanced. However, sufficient progress has been made in all three areas to warrant considering their future impact.

THE EFFECT OF INFORMATION TECHNOLOGY
ON MIDDLE MANAGERS

In 1958 Leavitt and Whisler[1] made some predictions about the effects of information technology on the role of middle managers. Their predic-

---

[1]H. J. Leavitt and T. L. Whisler, "Management in the 1980's," *Harvard Business Review,* Vol. 36 (November-December 1958), pp. 41–48.

tions were based on the state of the art of the time, and were seen as coming to fruition in the 1980s. In summary, they predicted the following:

1. Advances in information technology will result in planning and control functions becoming more centralized at the top echelons of the organization. Planning and control functions will centralize in the hands of information technology specialists.

2. Many middle manager positions will diminish in stature and value to the extent that planning and control functions are taken out of these positions. Concurrently, many middle manager positions will become more highly programmed and subject to more external control.

3. The line between top and middle management will be drawn more clearly and rigidly than it is now. This sharper line essentially will distinguish between management functions—planning, controlling, and implementing (carrying out plans devised by others).

Leavitt and Whisler predicted that widespread applications of information technology would practically do away with middle management as we knew it in 1958. Their predictions are based on the development of models that simulate the operations of the organizations and on the use of these models for planning, decision making, and controlling purposes. Since 1958 information technology has been used extensively, but it does not appear that this technology has produced the changes suggested by Leavitt and Whisler. Although it is probably too early to dismiss their predictions, it is of value to examine what impact information technology has had on middle managers and what the future impact might be.

Dearden,[2] in a very pertinent discussion about the possible fallacies and misconceptions in the use of information technology, also provides a good statement of the general categories of systems which are prevalent in business organizations. The general types of systems that he identifies are:

1. *Financial accounting and control.* These systems include financial statements, budgets, cost analyses, and so forth.

2. *Logistics systems.* These systems control the flow of materials from initial purchasing through the manufacture of the finished product. This system is manufacturing oriented.

3. *Marketing systems.* These systems deal with product lines, sales forecasting, advertising and promotion, and product planning.

[2]J. Dearden, "MIS Is a Mirage," *Harvard Business Review* (January-February 1972), pp. 90–99.

4. *Staff support systems.* These systems deal with personnel data and the data needs of other staff groups such as legal and public relations.

5. *R&D systems.* These are systems which support the R&D effort.

The earliest systems efforts were in financial accounting and control. Basically, the justification for computers in these areas was that the machines could do the work, at less cost, of large numbers of clerical personnel and provide a more useful flow of information in the process. The capacity of the machines for data, the versatility with which they could rearrange it, and the speed with which they could process it were cited as significant improvements over other machine methods or typical clerical efforts.

The financial accounting and control systems have several potential effects on the middle manager. By providing him with more specific data about his performance in a shorter time interval, he has better feedback. On the other hand, his superiors also get the same feedback. In a sense, the manager is then under closer scrutiny and is susceptible to closer controls from the top. The value of such feedback, of course, will depend on how it is used (see Chapter 7).

Logistics systems, in addition to providing feedback on performance, also establish the procedures the middle manager is to follow in doing certain aspects of his job and impose rigid time and data quality disciplines upon him. Thus the logistics system is an operating system that the middle manager is expected to follow. The impact of logistics systems on middle managers can best be seen from a situation which I had the occasion to study.

This particular logistics system supported a large-scale manufacturing operation with a complex product mix. It had the following overall sequence:

1. An overall manufacturing plan was developed to meet customer requirements.
2. Specific requirements then were placed on in-house component shops, assembly shop, and the purchasing organization to secure parts from external vendors.
3. The purchasing organization receives and inspects parts from vendors and places them in the manufacturing inventory.
4. The financial organization is notified of this receipt of satisfactory parts and pays the vendors.

This general sequence of events was supported by appropriate data input mechanisms, various status and control reports, and documentation to support payment to vendors. It was the first attempt at such a large-scale integrated system and was regarded as an ambitious one.

In general, it was found that the system was integrated but that the organization was not and thus had great difficulty in handling the demands of the increased flow of information. The following problems and attitudes were identified:

1. The various departments of the organization were concerned only with their own part of the system. They did not see themselves as part of a larger system and were not concerned about its overall success. This was true particularly at lower organization levels.

2. Organizations did not adapt themselves to the requirements of the system. In many instances relatively minor organization changes or changes in responsibility would have improved the system operation. Many organizations either did not see the need to adapt or, in some instances, showed marked unwillingness to make necessary changes. In general, the overall system was jeopardized because the various organizations did not or would not look beyond the goals and values that normally guided them.

3. Conflict between organizations increased, particularly where the inputs from one organization resulted in high error output to other organizations. In these cases there was considerable backbiting and finger-pointing as well as numerous memos being written for the "file" to later prove that one was correct.

4. Errors, made either by users or as a result of system design or hardware, had a very negative impact on the organization. Errors, and the inability to correct errors in particular, resulted in frustration and antagonism toward system designers and the system.

5. The role and credibility of the systems organization were challenged. In this organization the systems effort was centralized, and the systems people exerted considerable influence on the logic and procedure of the systems as well as on priorities. The resistance to the systems organization actually started during the design effort. Managers, in particular, resisted certain procedures, even though they were needed by the logic of the entire system, and were resentful when their particular area received low priority effort. When the system went on the line, the initial problems were used as further evidence to justify previously held opinions of the systems organization.

What was seen in the installation of this system is not unusual. The middle managers find that a large-scale system tends to disrupt the normal pattern of their lateral relationships. The "rules" by which the work flow is governed are more rigid, the private deals to evade the rules are more difficult to consummate, and the discipline, both personally and by the employees in this organization, needed to operate the system is more demanding and unforgiving.

Middle managers also are confronted with a new source of power and control with which to contend: the systems organization—particularly if it is centralized. Once an organization decides to go the management information systems route, it then becomes committed to a systems organization of some stature. One of the key impacts of the systems organization is on the work flow processes and attendant systems which cut across the middle management ranks. The logic and requirements of the system will either predominate or be strongly felt in the middle management ranks. In many respects, the systems organization dictates what will be done or, at a minimum, reconfirms current practices. Thus at times the middle managers may feel that they are being pushed in certain directions or that approval for their methods of operation depend upon the "new force," the systems organization.

The systems organization affects the middle manager in other ways. He is subject to the time input demands of the system as well as to data input quality standards. Errors tend to be highlighted, and he may no longer have a manual backup system available to him. In addition, he is now dependent on the systems organization for technical support. If he needs a systems or a systems revision, the assignment of a person to do the work and a priority are made by the systems organization in light of the organization needs. Thus, from his limited point of view, the middle manager may feel that he is not being supported when he feels he needs support and that he has no alternative resources.

From the top management point of view, logistics systems, in addition to hoped-for economics, potentially provide another means of insuring that their intentions are being carried out. The systems provide them with more specific and timely feedback about the *status* of work relative to goals and the opportunity to intercede early in the emergence of a problem if they choose to do so. Presumably, the performance of middle managers is more visible and more susceptible to direction and control from above. Thus top management has at its disposal an early warning system and can engage in management by exception approaches more frequently.

Top management can also use systems to implement cost-saving business practices across an entire organization which were difficult to do without access to information. This can best be illustrated through an example of logistics systems for a large field service organization.

This field service organization supports a complex electromechanical product on a worldwide basis. The field service organization, in its attempts to provide the right replacement parts in the right place on a timely basis, felt that its inventory and associated costs were too high. Managers at each location were carrying too high an inventory in order to protect themselves from shortages.

Projections from past replacement history clearly indicated that the overinventory and exhortations and edicts to the field managers to bring their inventories into line were not productive. A system was designed to provide a lower inventory level in the field; it operated as follows: (1) changes in inventory were constantly monitored; (2) the nearest location of an available part was indicated; (3) the time to get the part from the closest office was indicated; (4) the part was dispatched to the office where it was needed; (5) the part was reordered for the inventory of the office from which it was dispatched.

This system, which operated on a worldwide basis, took approximately 18 months to implement. The biggest job in implementation was to convince the field managers of its value. First, they had to be convinced that it would work, that is, they would get parts on a timely basis. Second, they had to be convinced that the system was a tool to help them do a better job and was not a spy system. After some experience with the system, the field managers were convinced and considerable savings in inventory costs were realized.

In this case an obvious need to achieve a reduction in replacement part inventory costs on a worldwide basis was achieved through the use of an effective information system. Wisely, top management recognized and made provision for dealing with the concerns of the field managers who would operate the system.

At this point in time, the Leavitt and Whisler predictions regarding the displacement of middle managers by information technology do not seem to have come true, although the potential for some displacement is there. At present, information technology appears to be directed toward substituting machine effort for human effort and toward providing an integrated flow of information that parallels the work flow. The integrated information flow is useful as an early warning system and for checking on the status of work efforts. In some instances systems have been designed specifically to implement good business practices. Whether or not their predictions will come true depends on a number of factors:

1. *A valid justification for automation.* In theory it might be possible to displace a great deal of middle manager effort by information technology. The question then arises of why do it. Would it result in a more effective organization? Would it eliminate some serious problems

in the organization? The decision to automate middle management is not inevitable but probably will be based on the same considerations used to automate other work areas. Usually these decisions are based on cost, productivity, and convenience considerations. If the cost of automation is offset by increased productivity and reduced cost, then the decision to automate is straightforward. In other instances, it may be justified for convenience, such as elimination of a problem. For example, if middle managers were to become a serious enough problem to top management in terms of attitudes and performance, one way top management could deal with the problem would be to automate as much of the middle management functions as possible. In any event, we should not be automating just for the sake of automating.

2. *State of the art.* As in all attempts at automation, the state of the art is a limiting factor. In information technology the basic state of the art requirements are models that simulate the operation of the organization, computer capacity, and access to both input and output. Of the three, the simulation models are the limiting factor, mostly because of the sheer number and complexity of the variables involved. Computer capacity does not appear to be a limiting problem as evolutions in hardware have stressed growth of capacity. Access has been aided materially by development of minicomputers, remote access units, and point of sale input devices.

Regardless of how far the state of the art is pushed, there will still be some need for subjective judgment. For example, one product manager indicated to me that he has available to him, through a remote terminal, a program which enables him to evaluate variations in shipment schedules against such various parameters as sales and profit budgets. Thus in any given month if he wanted to maximize the contribution of shipments to a profit budget, the program would indicate the ideal product mix to ship during that month. The problem is that there are many months when decisions regarding the product mix are highly subjective, for example, the decision to ship to a very annoying customer just to get him off your back.

3. *Behavioral reactions to systems.* System flowcharts inherently tend to be quite detailed and logical. One of the implied messages in these analyses is that if "everyone does what is expected of him as determined by the systems people, then we should get the predicted results." This is a reflection of the production methods engineering mentality to management positions. The evidence of negative reactions by production employees to end products of these methods is voluminous. Anyone who designs management systems without regard for the behavioral reactions

of the managers, at best, has to be regarded as incredibly naïve. Yet such systems are being designed.

From a behavioral point of view we can look at a management system as a design for a new social structure in an organization because any system creates roles, status and pay differentials, and potentialities for satisfying or frustrating important human needs. All too often, a system is designed and implemented without regard for the social-psychological characteristics of the current management process, with the result of more disruption and resistance than the organization can cope with. The outcome is usually the abandonment of a new system or, at best, less effective results. We do not know enough about how to implement new, large-scale systems on top of old, large-scale systems. The behavioral reactions are complex, but we are certain they are there.

In addition to the disruptive behavioral reactions to systems, there is another question. Do we really want management systems that potentially could result in highly programmed and routinized managerial tasks? Do we want to take out of managerial tasks the opportunities for innovation, creativity, flexibility, and human satisfaction as we have done in far too many clerical and production jobs? Taken to its extreme limits, management systems could do this.

At the present time, we have to conclude that information technology applications in the middle management ranks are at an early and somewhat primitive stage. At best, they offer the middle manager a tool to eliminate some of the information accumulation and processing drudgery from his job and a more meaningful data base on which to conduct his lateral relationships. At this stage of information technology, the middle managers may feel somewhat more constrained by the requirements of the system and more exposed to their peers and top management in terms of their performance. It is not unreasonable, then, to expect them to feel somewhat uncomfortable with information technology at this point.

BEHAVIORAL SCIENCE TECHNOLOGY
IN OTHER PARTS OF THE ORGANIZATION

Some of the most innovative and potentially productive applications of behavioral science technology are those involving clerical and production employees. If these innovations, which generally fall under the heading of job enrichment and participative management, should result in permanent changes in these segments of the workforce, then they will have a significant impact on the role of the middle manager.

Walton has reported on what is perhaps the most significant application of behavioral science technology to a work organization in the United States. This application, in a new pet food factory, is similar to a number of such applications in European countries where participative approaches generally have received greater attention. Walton reports the following design features of the work system:[3]

Preparation of the start-up team. For approximately two years prior to the start-up of the new plant, the nucleus of the management for the new plant analyzed alternative forms of work organization in the light of available behavioral science technology and the needs of the workforce. They also visited other companies to observe innovative behavioral science applications. This preparation provided a frame of reference and a sense of commitment in the start-up team for more innovative ways of organizing the work in their new plant.

Autonomous work groups. The plant consisted of approximately 70 employees who were divided into work teams of 7 to 14 members and a work leader. Each shift had one work team responsible for processing and one responsible for packaging. Each person in the group had a set of assigned tasks for which he had primary responsibility. Tasks could be shared by individuals and also reassigned based on an individual's interests and skills. The assignment of tasks was by team consensus, and team members also were involved in dealing with problems within their group or with other groups, redistribution of tasks to cover for absent employees, selecting new team members and team members to serve on plantwide committees, and in counseling team members who did not meet team standards.

Integrated support functions and challenging job assignments. Insofar as possible, staff functions and other specialized jobs were incorporated into the jobs of team members. Team members performed almost all maintenance on the machines they operated, performed the housekeeping in their areas, conducted quality tests, and screened job applicants for their team. Thus the team members had an opportunity to perform a wide variety of enriching tasks and shared the menial ones. Deliberate attempts were made to eliminate drill or routine work and to balance such work in a job with more challenging tasks.

Mobility and pay based on learning. A unique innovation in this plant was to base mobility and pay increases on the number of jobs learned. Thus an employee could increase his pay by learning new skills rather than by progressing through a job hierarchy.

[3]R. E. Walton, "How to Counter Alienation in the Plant," *Harvard Business Review* (November-December 1972), pp. 70–81.

Facilitative leadership and information sharing. The team leaders were responsible for team development and group decision making as opposed to the traditional planning, directing, and controlling functions. They were supported in this role by a downward sharing of relevant business information and decision-making parameters. Thus many decisions now could be made at the operator level.

Plant rules evolved from the needs of the organization and its members. The management nucleus did not establish any work rules in advance of the plant opening. Rather, the rules evolved as a result of operating experience.

Uniform physical and social environment. Traditional status symbols (parking, entrances, decor) were minimized in order to deemphasize status differentials in the plant.

Commitment to change. Management made a commitment to continually assess the productivity of the plant and its relevance to employee needs, and thus they anticipated learning from their experience and implementing appropriate changes.

In Western Europe these kinds of innovations are more commonplace, particularly in Scandinavia. Participative approaches in Western Europe generally are called industrial democracy and are based on legislation designed to give employees greater influence. In Germany this approach is known as "Mitbestimmung"; it gives labor and management equality on supervisory boards in the steel and coal industries and minority positions in other industries.

Thorsrud and Emery[4] have described the evolution and operation of industrial democracy in Norway. It started in Norway around World War I with a law that established work councils in companies to deal with matters of mutual interest to labor and management. After World War II, industrial democracy agreements were extended to include being informed and consulted about major company affairs in addition to the right to organize and bargain for wages and about conditions of work. Generally, this led to a pattern of employee representation on various management committees. An examination of this type of representation through management committees suggested it was not having much of an impact in the production area. The feeling arose that participation through elected representatives on committees would have to be supplemented by *meaningful opportunities for participation by the employee in his work area.* This then led to a series of experiments in which jobs and work roles were restructured to provide greater participation.

[4]E. Thorsrud and F. E. Emery, "Industrial Democracy in Norway," *Industrial Relations* (February 1970), pp. 187–196.

The types of changes that have been made as a result of the extension of the industrial democracy concept to the work place are very significant. The increased authority and decision making of production employees, to a large extent, has been derived from the first-line supervisor's job. In the case of the pet food plant the team leader's role is to help the team members to make decisions, and in other organizations the first-line supervisors' position has been phased out.

What will be the impact of this form of organization on the middle management structure? While there has not been much documentation, we can report some personal observations. We have referred frequently to the middle managers' role as implementers and coordinators. If the primary work groups become capable of assuming more of these functions, what is left for the middle managers? Depending on the type of technology and size of the organization, there will be quite a bit for middle managers to do. First, as in the case of the team leaders in the pet food plant, a large segment of their role will be as facilitators. They will have to establish a climate for participation in their respective organizations and help the team members to become proficient in their expanded roles. Second, in larger organizations, they will continue to perform coordinating functions which are not practical for team members to do. And third, in organizations with complex product or manufacturing technologies, the middle manager will serve as a key technical resource to the team members.

What little experience I have had in organizations that have innovated in a significant way with participative management or industrial democracy suggests that middle managers are not particularly overjoyed with it. Basically, they see it as a threat to their own position and status. They can point to the reduced numbers or the changed role of first-line supervisors and by extrapolation see what might happen to them. They view the downward thrust of authority and decision making from them to the production teams as particularly threatening—especially if it is not compensated by an increased delegation of responsibility and information flow from their superiors to them. "When my boss does it, I'll do it," is a good summary of their feelings. In France, the reactions of middle managers to attempts at industrial democracy were described to me as follows:

> In this movement, the middle managers have been left aside. They are now starting to ask for a more important part in the managerial decisions. Once again, this movement (by the middle managers) is collectively organized, and is favored by the Ministry of Labor and Social Relations.

What we are saying is that the middle managers, for reasons which make sense to them, can be a significant barrier to the implementation of participative management unless the participative management approaches also are responsive to their needs. If participative innovation enhances their roles to the extent that it has done in the limited applications to production groups, then their resistance should evaporate. Middle managers, of course, are key collaborators in any innovations affecting themselves and others, and their attitudes are instrumental to the success of such innovation. In other words, they are in a key position to "make or break" such attempts. This points up the need to do some work with middle managers along the lines suggested in Chapters 6, 7, and 8 prior to any serious attempts to innovate at lower levels. This is particularly true in older and larger organizations where the problems in the middle management ranks are apt to be more complex and of longer duration.

INNOVATIONS IN THE USE OF ORGANIZATION STRUCTURE

We have called this section innovations in the use of organization structure as opposed to innovations in organization structure because there have been few practical innovations in organization structure. In any event, organization structure does not produce results, per se; its value is in *how* it is used. In this section, in particular, we will examine the uses of matrix organizations in respect to the middle manager's role and the problems associated with it.

The matrix organization goes one step beyond the traditional functional organization in that it provides an additional focus on major customers, projects, products, or problems. For example, in the case of a large military R&D project, an organization may be established to manage the project and to provide the direct interface with the customer. The project management negotiates the technical and business matters with the customer and then uses and monitors the functional resources in the total organization to get the work done. In some cases there may be two or three such major project organizations operating at the same time and which are making simultaneous use of the functional resources in the organization. This type of arrangement is illustrated in Figure 5

As can be seen, the term *matrix* derives from the arrangement of projects in rows and the functions in columns. As you move across any row, the particular project draws upon the resources of the different functions to help meet its commitments. Going down a column, the function is responsible to several projects. In marketing organizations,

5. Matrix organization.

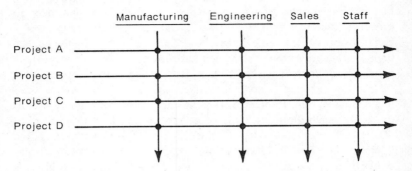

it is not uncommon to find product managers with responsibility for a product or product line representing the rows and the various internal functions representing the columns. This arrangement clearly identifies the point of responsibility for the product which would not exist if the organization structure were purely functional in nature.

Over and above the obvious marketing and responsibility assignment advantages of the matrix organization, it offers a broader variety of roles and more opportunities for movement for the middle manager. The jobs along the rows typically offer opportunities for persons with entrepreneurial or business management interests, as these positions typically involve developing business or marketing strategies, pricing, customer interfacing, and integrating the efforts of functional organizations. In a miniature sense, these positions can offer a total business experience. For the individual who has come up through a functional organization and is now boxed in, a lateral movement to a product or project organization can offer an opportunity to expand his skills as well as to get a broader view of how a business operates.

In Figure 6 the career path possibilities in a matrix organization have been diagrammed; we will use a salesman to demonstrate the possible moves. On the right is the sales organization, which is functional; on the left is the product management organization, which is business oriented. Above these segments is the general management of the total marketing organization. The salesman enters at point A and in time is promoted to a district sales manager (point B). In the typical functional organization his next upward promotion opportunity would be to regional sales manager (point C) where he could become boxed in. However, the existence of the product organization offers him opportunities for additional moves, without the necessity of being promoted. For example,

6. Development moves in a matrix organization.

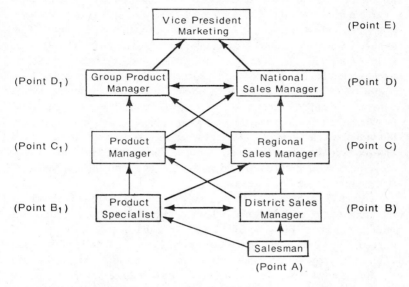

(Point E)

(Point D₁)   Group Product Manager   National Sales Manager   (Point D)

(Point C₁)   Product Manager   Regional Sales Manager   (Point C)

(Point B₁)   Product Specialist   District Sales Manager   (Point B)

Salesman

(Point A)

he can go from point B, district sales manager, to point B₁, product specialist. From point B₁ he can move up to product manager, point C₁, to point C, regional manager, or even back to point B, but to a larger district. The zigzagging and lateral moves not only offer more opportunities for movement but opportunities for increased learning. It also means that the individual who has made a number of such moves, and has demonstrated success at each level, is much better prepared to move into general marketing management (points D, D₁, and E).

The same advantages and strategies would also exist in large R&D efforts which are organized in matrix form. The young engineer, for example, could take on several functional assignments and then move into the project management group and then back out to another functional assignment. Of course there are other possible variations depending on the size and complexity of the effort, but the point again is that the matrix organization offers more opportunity for movement and learning. The young engineer who has designed components in a functional organization, has interfaced with the customer, and has been exposed to a broader business point of view in the project organization and then moved back to the functional group cannot help but be a better designer or manager in a functional area as a result of the broader exposure.

These examples reflect relatively stable matrix organizations, that is, those in which the customer relationship or product effort is of relatively long duration. Auerbach[5] describes the use of the matrix organization in an environment where it was important to establish strong customer interfaces and where the customers changed relatively frequently. This application was in a computer consulting firm which he heads. He went from a hierarchically structured, straight-line, geographically organization to a modified matrix style that focused on key market areas.

Under the matrix concept as it applied to his organization, people who were available were assigned to projects with clients regardless of where the employee was located geographically. In other words, the individual was assigned to a project where his or her skills were needed and for as long as the skills were needed. This resulted in the continual movement of employees in and out of projects and the formation of work teams as the need arose.

Auerbach's experiences in making the transition from the straight hierarchy to the modified matrix have some significant implications for middle managers. First, he found that some managers whose technical expertise had diminished and whose primary talent was administration were not happy with the new setup and left. Second, this attrition in the middle level supervisory ranks coincided with fewer levels of supervision in the matrix organization and less need for supervisors. And third, many individuals who might have been promoted to middle manager to justify higher salaries could be paid these salaries, based primarily on high-level technical skills and the ability to contribute directly to projects. In effect, he reduced the overhead costs and made more technical effort available for direct billing. He also was able to get around a situation that is found all too frequently in many organizations: that of promoting a highly competent technical person to a middle manager position as a reward for his technical ability, with the result of having a poor manager and losing a good technical contributor.

There are other organization innovations which stress temporary membership in a work group based on the individual's particular skill and the needs of the situation. They generally tend to be variations and elaborations of the matrix organization and go under such headings as star and circle organizations. Again, these variations stress the use of an individual's skills in situations where he can contribute in accordance with his ability. Thus in some situations the individual may perform in a junior role and in other situations in a senior role. His status is

[5]I. L. Auerbach, "Changing from Hierarchy to Matrix," *Innovation* (March 1972), pp. 22–29.

not determined by where he is in the hierarchy but by what he can contribute in a situation.

The matrix organization and its variations have significant implications for middle managers:

1. It reduces the need for middle managers because the hierarchy tends to be reduced and because they offer more opportunities to pay individuals for technical performance rather than promoting them to middle manager status in order to reward them.
2. It provides more opportunities for lateral moves to relieve the boxing-in problem and moves that give middle managers a broader business perspective.
3. It provides more instrinsically satisfying jobs in that the individual is closer to and contributing more directly to a problem, product, or customer. It also offers more variety.

The matrix and temporary forms of organizations, while offering significant advantages, do create a new set of problems that has to be dealt with. The interpersonal scenario in matrix organizations reads along the following lines. The project groups have the prime customer interface and responsibility for satisfying the customer. They are highly dependent on the performance of the functional groups in order to meet their objectives. On the other hand, they do not have any direct authority over the functional groups. Rather, they negotiate for their services and at times are in direct competition with other project teams for these services. Of course, they provide the money to man the functional organizations and are constrained by their budgeted commitments to the customer.

In this type of situation it is not unusual for the project organization to use their customer relationship and control over funds to exert unnecessary pressure on the functional groups. In fact, many project groups tend to look at the functional groups as working for them. This can distort the traditional status relationships in an organization and cause considerable disruptive conflict. If the projects are overzealous in measuring the performance of the functional groups, for example, large numbers of measurements or frequent and lengthy reviews, they can seriously impair the morale and performance of the functional contributors. In the extreme, the projects can exert pressures to have people fired and use this as a threat.

Davis[6] has used team-building approaches at TRW to deal with interor-

---

[6]S. Davis, "Building More Effective Teams," *Innovation* (October 1970), pp. 32–41.

ganizational problems that develop between project and functional groups. The OD approach is very similar to that described in Chapter 6 between the sales and manufacturing organizations. The purpose of the team-building OD approach is to eliminate the stereotypes that tend to develop between organizational components, to help the groups understand their mutual expectations, and to help them establish a more productive working relationship. I also have found that movement of people between project and functional organizations builds a better understanding of the different roles and facilitates cooperative effort.

In this chapter we have looked at three possible sources of change in the middle manager's job: information technology, advances in the behavioral sciences, and more innovative uses of organization structure. In order to provide an overview of the potential effects of these factors, they have been summarized in Table 6. Each source of change is listed along with three possible effects—to enhance, to diminish, to eliminate —they might have on the middle manager's job.

As can be seen, all of the sources of change have the potential effect of enhancing the middle manager's job. Information technology could enhance it by eliminating routine elements. In effect, it could represent a form of job enrichment. The behavioral science applications elsewhere in the organization also could lead to enrichment by having tasks now performed by middle managers done elsewhere. Innovations in the use of organization structure provide greater development opportunities and opportunities for lateral movement.

Information technology has the greatest potential for diminishing the middle manager's job. This would occur if systems were used to impose even tighter controls on middle managers, thus reducing their flexibility through increased programming of their activities.

If our goal is to provide more enhanced middle manager positions in the future, then we should be guided by the "enhance" column for each potential source of change. Thus information systems should be used to eliminate as much routine drudgery as possible from middle management positions, as well as designed as a tool for middle managers. This can be done in conjunction with behavioral science based methods and innovations in the use of organization structure.

One important point that emerges from Table 6 is the possibility that information technology and behavioral science based efforts can be carried on in ways that conflict. In our not too unusual state of organizational schizophrenia, it would not be unusual to find the systems people designing an information system that diminishes the middle manager's role,

Table 6. Effect of change on the middle manager's role

Potential Source of Change	Enhance	Diminish	Eliminate
Information technology Financial, accounting, and control systems	Could enhance the position if these data are given to middle managers as an aid in planning and for use as self-corrective feedback.	Would diminish the position if these data were used to over-control the middle manager and if performance results were used in a strongly punitive manner.	No effect.
Logistics systems	Could enhance the job by eliminating the chores associated with developing useful data; middle managers would have more time and a better basis for applying their judgment to situations.	The logic, constraints, and disciplines of the system could reduce the manager's flexibility. If the system were the tail that wagged the dog, then the middle manager's job definitely would be diminished.	To the extent that the job was enhanced by eliminating a significant amount of routine data chores, the middle manager's span could be increased, thereby resulting in fewer middle managers.
Behavioral science applications	Would free the manager from many activities that could be done at lower levels. Would introduce new elements into his role: facilitator, team developer.		Might result in the need for fewer middle managers as a significant portion of his tasks might be performed by others.
Innovations in the use of organization structure	Would provide more opportunities for lateral movement and growth.		Under certain conditions, matrix forms of organizations could result in elimination of middle levels in the hierarchy.

while the personnel people are attempting to implement innovations to enhance the middle manager's role. The important point to stress is that a technical system does have social and interpersonal implications and that the technical design should reflect desired social and interpersonal objectives.

Each source of change also appears to have the potential of reducing the number of middle management positions. This raises the question of whether we should consciously strive to reduce the number of middle managers. I think the answer to this question is a resounding *yes!* The reduction of the number of middle managers would have several distinct advantages:

Reduce complexity. The complexity of lateral relationships potentially goes up by a function of $\frac{[n\,(n-1)]}{2}$, where *n* is the number of interfaces between middle managers. Of course, not all the potential interfaces result in actual interactions, but the interactions do go up as the number of middle managers increases, and inevitably we put in another level of middle managers. This, of course, produces additional complexity in the hierarchy. Thus, it stands to reason that fewer middle managers means fewer interfaces and less complexity.

The remaining jobs can be enhanced. With fewer middle manager positions and success in eliminating a lot of the routine in these jobs, there is a significant opportunity to enhance the remaining jobs through different methods of enrichment.

Only persons with managerial potential would be middle managers. If there were fewer middle manager positions, top management could be more selective in terms of who is promoted to the middle management ranks. They could also stop promoting individuals to the middle management ranks for the wrong reasons, such as a reward for technical competence, as these individuals will have more appropriate opportunities for their skills.

It is always nice to contemplate the future because we can paint optimistic pictures and not be immediately concerned with results. There is an optimistic picture in the future for middle managers. To get to the future we, of course, must start with the present, and it is at this point that reality reenters the picture. Any improvements we make in the future inevitably will depend on how effective we are in dealing with our current middle management situations.

chapter ten

The Initiatives for Change

IN THIS BOOK we have considered the situation of a relatively small segment of the workforce—the middle managers. Although they are a small group, their position in the hierarchy makes them critically important. As the gatekeepers between top management and the rest of the organization, and as the coordinators of the goal-directed activities of the organization, the performance of the middle managers can make the difference between a mediocre or excellent organization. In this chapter we consider some practical processes through which an organization can start to examine the middle manager environment.

CHANGE THROUGH TOP MANAGEMENT

In hierarchical organizations the initiatives for major changes traditionally rest in top management. Before they make any commitment for change, most top managements want some indicators as to the nature and extent of middle management problems in their own organizations. Some top managements may want to ease into the problem by studying it first in a way which does not arouse a lot of expectations. If no significant problems are found, then the matter can be dropped. If significant problems are identified, then additional explorations can be made and followed by corrective courses of action. There are a number of ways that top management can take the initiative in exploring the middle management situation in their organization. The following methods vary in terms of effort required, visibility of the effort, and the implied commitment to continue the explorations.

CRITICAL INCIDENT METHOD

A good place to start is for top managers to state their perceptions of the middle management organization in some organized fashion. This can be done simply by asking each top manager to give his opinions or to cite the pluses and minuses they see in the operation of the middle management organization.

To be more systematic, they can use the "critical incident method" to collate their perceptions. With this method top managers are asked to develop eight to ten specific incidents which represent examples of *effective* and *ineffective* middle manager performance. In developing these incidents top management should select examples of performance which are indicative of exceptionally good or exceptionally poor performance in the middle management organization. The incident should be described in behavioral terms, that is, what the middle manager did or did not do, and should also include the consequences of the behavior.

The following are examples of critical incidents for middle managers in a national sales organization.

Effective performance—regional manager. A regional manager deliberately transferred high potential salesmen out of areas where there were several such salesmen. These men were sent to divisions with fewer high potential salesmen, so it was possible for the local division manager to concentrate development opportunities upon them. In addition, the regional manager transferred some of his stronger salesmen into divisions with weak sales records in order to beef up their strength. Most of these moves involved relocations, and the regional manager did not passively accept the talent distributions that he happened to encounter, especially when this was maldistributed according to his needs.

Ineffective performance—product manager. A salesman developed a complete package for marketing and advertising a certain product, and presented these in detail to a product director and his staff. He received little or no feedback at the session, not even the courtesy of a thank you. He revised the package and went back with the second presentation, and again was simply heard out without getting any reaction. The implication was that the product director felt that this was his bailiwick and he did not want to have any outside interference.

Top managers can collect such incidents with minimal help from a staff person or a consultant and then categorize the incidents according to major themes. The value of the information is that it provides a collective view of the middle management organization, at least as seen by top management. The results can be reviewed for major areas of effectiveness and ineffectiveness in the middle management ranks and a decision can then be made for further exploration and in what areas.

TURNOVER ANALYSIS

A second method that involves low visibility is to examine the turnover patterns in the organization. Exit interviews of middle managers are of some use here, but more revealing data can be obtained by contacting the terminee approximately six months *after* he has left. The terminee can be sent a questionnaire with questions relating to his reasons for leaving, perceptions of the organization, and so on. A suitable cover letter explaining the purpose of the questionnaire and soliciting cooperation should be included. The data from such questionnaires tend to provide much more insight into the reasons for leaving than information given at the exit interview. Again, these data can be analyzed for significant themes and provide a basis for additional planning and action.

Some statistical analysis of turnover also should be pursued. Total attrition rates tend to mask a great deal of meaningful information; therefore it is important to look beyond the gross turnover rates for middle managers. For example, is the turnover concentrated around a few positions or in a certain age group? The use of such parameters can produce more specific and meaningful insights into the turnover patterns.

Another way to deal with turnover data is to divide the terminees into several categories: "those we hate to see go and will miss," "those whom we will not miss," and "all others." The first and second groups should be compared in terms of specific parameters such as age, position, education, and stated reason for leaving. For those in the first group, the question also might be asked, "What might we have done differently to prevent this person from leaving?"

A significant part of the turnover analysis is to study those areas where there is little turnover. In other words, look at middle management positions where little or no turnover takes place and assess the significance of the low turnover. Is it an older group? Is it a position that boxes in managers? Does its low turnover prevent significant career moves for others? Quite frequently, such patterns do emerge and lend themselves to corrective actions.

SURVEYS

A survey is a more direct and comprehensive method for diagnosing a problem situation, and also represents a greater commitment to action. The very act of the survey usually is taken as an indication of interest, with an implied commitment to do something. This is a key point when considering a survey. In many instances top management would like to have the information, as well as the option to avoid commitment to follow up if they believe none is warranted. In respect to this point the best top management can expect in a survey is to maintain some control over the follow-up action that is taken. In some survey approaches, to be described below, top management can even wind up with minimal control over the action to be taken. Surveys, then, do require serious thought because they raise expectations for change. If there is reluctance to change, surveys are best avoided, as unfilled expectations can exacerbate existing problems and lower the credibility of top management.

A number of available survey approaches will be described briefly.

Questionnaire surveys are perhaps the most widely used. Typically, they consist of a series of statements describing the work environment, job, pay, benefits, and so on, and the respondent is asked to indicate the extent of his agreement-disagreement or satisfaction-dissatisfaction with each. The questions may be supplemented with some open-ended questions that allow the person to express an opinion in his own words. In addition, certain demographic data are asked for—age, length of service, education, department, exempt versus nonexempt status—to aid in the analysis.

The advantages of the questionnaire survey are its uniformity, ease of administration (no more than one hour in most cases and can be done in large groups), amenability to computer analysis and quantification, and flexibility in categorizing and analyzing the data. Its limitation, however, is that interpretation of the meaning behind the data is sometimes difficult. A typical questionnaire survey for middle managers is shown in the appendix.

Interview surveys involve interviewing employees individually or in small groups. It is a more expensive procedure and usually not amenable to quantification. This kind of survey, however, can provide powerful insights into the problems in an organization. The key, of course, is in the skill of the interviewer. Highly skilled interviewers usually can probe deeply into an issue and follow up on significant leads. If top management should opt for an interview survey, then particular attention should be given to the selection of skilled interviewers.

Quite frequently, it is possible to *combine the interview and questionnaire approaches* and gain the advantages of both. For example, a random sample of employees can be interviewed first. These data can provide many of the insights that come from interview surveys and also provide input for writing appropriate questionnaire items, that is, that tap the major concerns of employees. These items then can be supplemented by points that are of interest to top management. In effect, the combined approach provides a custom-designed survey with the power of both.

A typical end result of surveys—questionnaire or interview—is for the data to be collected and analyzed and for recommendations for follow-up action to be made to top management. At this point many survey efforts bog down. Top management frequently becomes defensive about the results and attempts to minimize their significance. The recommendations are often attacked as being inappropriate or unrealistic.

In some organizations this problem is minimized by putting the responsibility for developing, administering, interpreting, recommending, and implementing follow-up action in the hands of a team of employees. In this approach top management expresses a great deal of confidence in its employees and relinquishes excessive control of how the survey results will be used. For further details on the methods and results of this kind of approach, see the articles by Myers[1] and Truell.[2]

ORGANIZATION DEVELOPMENT (OD)

In Chapter 6 we discussed the use of OD methods to increase the mutual understanding and interpersonal relationships between top and middle management and within the middle manager group itself. In the context of this chapter OD represents a significant initiative for change by top management and a commitment on its part to deal directly with the issues and the people involved, with no preconceived notions about solutions. If top management does have preconceptions, then, at a minimum, it recognizes that these ideas will be open to scrutiny and subject to change by inputs in OD sessions.

For a top management that is steeped in authoritarian traditions, OD represents a radical change in style and relationships, and many are reluctant to use it. Others consider OD after all else has failed, while others realize that time, effort, and, at times, personal discomfort is worth it in terms of an organization that can direct more of its energies toward dealing with important business matters in an integrated manner. All this is a way of saying that OD is a powerful technique for change but an approach which should not be prescribed lightly. A key to a successful OD effort is the willingness of top management to enter into a process that could change their roles. If they cannot make this commitment then they best stay away from major OD efforts.

[1]M. S. Myers, *Every Employee a Manager*. New York: McGraw-Hill, 1971.
[2]G. F. Truell, "Using Mini-Surveys to Start the Problem-Solving Process," *Personnel Journal* (July 1970).

CHANGE THROUGH MIDDLE MANAGEMENT

Another focus for initiating change in the middle manager ranks is, of course, the middle managers themselves. At the present time they seem to be handicapped. They are a small and widely dispersed group and they do not appear to have an organized base through which to exert leverage. According to AMA's survey, *Manager Unions?*, the middle managers are not optimistic about the top management's response to the idea of discussing conditions of employment on even an *informal basis* with middle manager groups. Fifty-five percent of the middle managers felt that top management would strongly oppose the idea. They also are somewhat fearful of this approach: 48 percent feared reprisals (by top management) would thwart attempts to organize informal middle management groups.

The low initiative level of the middle managers to change their own situation is not surprising and quite explainable.

1. Any attempts by middle managers to take initiatives against top management takes on the aura of "biting the hand that feeds you." And keep in mind that middle managers have no legal protection to undertake such initiatives as forming unions. They can organize if they wish to, but there are no unfair labor practices associated with the refusal of top management to bargain with them. Thus top management clearly has fate control over the middle managers, and the middle managers are somewhat reluctant to tempt fate.

2. A second factor is the very role of middle managers and the expectations inherent in their roles. They, after all, are there to carry out the intentions of top management, and to do otherwise is incongruent.

3. The widely dispersed middle managers are just beginning to recognize that they share some significant problems and concerns. I see this shock of recognition quite clearly and frequently in sessions with middle managers where their problems are being discussed. The realization by a middle manager that "that's me you're talking about and I'm not the only one with these problems" can be quite startling. Initially, it removes the burden from the middle manager of feeling that the problems he is experiencing, somehow, are a result of his incompetence. He also begins to see the organization factors involved and the possibilities for changes to improve his situation. In many respects, this recognition can be likened to the early stages of consciousness raising wherein a person recognizes that he or she shares certain problems with others and that the conditions creating the problems can be and should be eliminated. This, of course, could lead to greater militancy and initiative to bring about change.

There is some evidence that individually middle managers are reacting to their environment. Job and career changes, refusals of promotions, and redirection of effort described in Chapter 3 represent the denial or withholding of effort to their employing organization. If this attitude becomes widespread, then top management will be faced with a serious problem, as the odds are that the middle managers who would go this route will be the better ones. Top management then will be forced either to deal with mass mediocrity in the middle management ranks or to change the environment to keep and attract the better ones.

CHANGE THROUGH THIRD PARTIES

Interested "third parties" are a third source of initiative. Counted among the third parties are union leaders, behavioral scientists who specialize in organizational problems, and government.

At best, the interest of *union leaders* in organizing middle managers is lukewarm. Union leaders are not banking on top management to voluntarily recognize middle manager unions, nor do they feel that the middle managers have enough organized power to bring about a change in the law that would require mandatory recognition of middle manager unions.

The *behavioral scientists* who specialize in organizational problems do represent a significant source of initiative for change. Their scientific disciplines enable them to identify problems, to conduct research which provides new knowledge, and to develop more appropriate manpower management practices. The behavioral scientists also have been strong advocates for change as well as activists in consciousness raising for certain issues such as job enrichment.

Likert, Herzberg, Argyris, and Gellerman are well known within many organizations, yet each works from the outside. Thus they are quite free to tell it like it is without the usual concerns one might have about speaking out as a member of an organization. Innovations originating in the behavioral sciences are receiving more attention in organizations. Everyday we learn more about the practical uses of such innovations as job enrichment, OD, and participative management. In respect to the middle managers, we are just beginning to see the start of external consciousness raising and advocacy roles.

The role of *government* is somewhat less clear and more distant. In recent years government has been very active in bringing about changes in manpower policies and practices. Equal employment opportunity and safety legislation are two examples. There is no doubt that significant change has and will continue to occur as a result of these legislative actions. Some may regard the changes as too slow, while others see them as oppressive. We will not debate this point here but merely emphasize that government action has resulted in change.

Now, in respect to middle managers, there is little likelihood that we will see specific *legislation* directed at their needs. Rather, we might expect middle managers to benefit from legislation that is directed at the total workforce. One possible area for legislation is pensions. More flexible arrangements in the form of portable pensions would be of considerable value to middle managers in that it would enable them to change jobs more readily. In effect, the middle manager could build up a pension nest egg, much as university professors do, regardless of the number of employers he had and without highly restrictive service requirements.

Another possible area of legislation has to do with the quality of work as it pertains to job satisfaction. Legislative hearings have been held to explore the problems of worker dissatisfaction but as yet no specific legislation has been proposed. We can, however, engage in a modest flight of fancy and try to imagine what it's going to be like on the day when organizations are asked to submit data showing compliance with a set of standards guaranteeing each and every employee—middle managers as well—an enriched and satisfying job! Of course, this is fanciful, but it is clear that the government has made significant impact on work practices in difficult areas. If past experience is any guideline, then we should expect it to want to expand this area.

There is no doubt in my mind that the problems in the middle management ranks are of sufficient number and intensity to represent a crisis. The problems represent a crisis in the sense that middle managers are turned off in large and growing numbers and that they are not being allowed to meet their potential in their organizations. There is growing recognition that serious problems, if not a crisis, do exist, but, at the moment, the problems are just sitting there. No one seems to be doing much about them. Perhaps it has to boil over before some initiatives are taken.

Of course, the key question is "Who will take the initiative in dealing with the situation?"—a key question because the group that takes the initiative more than likely will determine the solution. If government takes the initiative, then we may find ourselves having to comply with legal guidelines assuring worker satisfaction. If the middle managers take the initiative as a group, then we may see pressures for legislation that would protect them if they chose to form manager unions. If the middle managers take the initiative individually, then we can expect more of them to withdraw or withhold their best efforts from their employing organizations. If top management takes the initiative, we might find ways of increasing the effectiveness and satisfaction of the middle management organization.

We are at a point where the serious nature of middle management problems is becoming apparent. No one as yet has taken the initiative to do something about these situations. This also means that at this point the outcome is not clear. And there the matter rests for now.

Appendix
Questionnaire Survey for Middle Managers

THIS APPENDIX CONTAINS 38 questionnaire items around which a survey for middle managers can be developed. Subjects such as facilities have not been considered as they tend to be quite specific to each organization. In the area of benefits (items 23 and 24), a format for questions is suggested. The specifics of the questions will, of course, depend on the particular benefits of the organization.

MANAGEMENT SURVEY

Top management is very much interested in understanding the people who work in the organization and their reactions to what they experience on their job. The information which you provide could play an important role in making XYZ Corporation a more effective organization and a better place for you to work.

What you say in this questionnaire is completely confidential. Any report that is made will be in the form of a general statistical summary. Your responses will have absolutely no bearing upon your employment or advancement.

We are interested in your opinion. Don't answer the questions how you think we want them answered, but as you really feel. Remember this is not a test. There are no right or wrong answers.

THANK YOU FOR YOUR COOPERATION

INSTRUCTIONS

1. Be sure to read all questions carefully.
2. Place a check (✔) next to response that best describes your feelings. Check only one response per question.
3. Remember, this is NOT A TEST. YOUR OPINION IS THE ONLY CORRECT ANSWER.

A. ROLE SATISFACTION

   1. How do you feel about the *type* of work you are doing in your present job?

     _____ It is exactly the type of work I want to be doing.

     _____ It is very much like the type of work I want to be doing.

     _____ It is somewhat like the type of work I want to be doing.

     _____ It is not very much like the type of work I want to be doing.

     _____ It is not at all like the type of work I want to be doing.

   2. I enjoy my spare-time activities much more than the work I do.

     _____ Strongly agree

     _____ Agree

     _____ Disagree

     _____ Strongly disagree

     _____ No opinion

   3. To me, my work is mainly a way of making money.

     _____ Strongly agree

     _____ Agree

     _____ Disagree

     _____ Strongly disagree

     _____ No opinion

   4. The work I do is one of the most satisfying parts of my life.

     _____ Strongly agree

     _____ Agree

     _____ Disagree

     _____ Strongly disagree

     _____ No opinion

5. My job offers me an opportunity to do varied and interesting work.

_____ Strongly agree

_____ Agree

_____ Disagree

_____ Strongly disagree

_____ No opinion

B. COMMUNICATIONS

6. I receive sufficient specific information relative to my immediate job to do it properly.

_____ Strongly agree

_____ Agree

_____ Disagree

_____ Strongly disagree

_____ No opinion

7. I receive sufficient information about company/division/department and operations as they relate to my activity.

_____ Strongly agree

_____ Agree

_____ Disagree

_____ Strongly disagree

_____ No opinion

8. Communication between the groups I have to work with is good.

_____ Strongly agree

_____ Agree

_____ Disagree

_____ Strongly disagree

_____ No opinion

9. Top management is usually well informed about current needs at my level.

_____ Strongly agree

_____ Agree

_____ Disagree

_____ Strongly disagree

_____ No opinion

C. JOB UNDERSTANDING AND APPRAISAL

10. I have a clear understanding of what my immediate manager expects of me on my job.

_____ Strongly agree

_____ Agree

_____ Disagree

_____ Strongly disagree

_____ No opinion

11. My manager has given me specific help in improving on my present job.

   _____ Strongly agree

   _____ Agree

   _____ Disagree

   _____ Strongly disagree

   _____ No opinion

12. My manager does a good job in discussing appraisals.

   _____ Strongly agree

   _____ Agree

   _____ Disagree

   _____ Strongly disagree

   _____ Don't know, have not had an appraisal discussion with him

13. How much help has your manager given you in planning your future job development?

   _____ Great deal

   _____ Some help

   _____ Very little

   _____ None

14. How worthwhile was your last performance-appraisal discussion in helping you to improve your performance?

   _____ Very worthwhile

   _____ Some value

   _____ Very little value

   _____ Never had discussion

D. JOB SECURITY

15. My future here is as secure as I can rightfully expect it to be.

   _____ Strongly agree

   _____ Agree

   _____ Disagree

   _____ Strongly disagree

   _____ No opinion

E. COMPENSATION

16. How do you feel the pay for your job compares with pay for similar work in *other* companies?

_____ Higher than any of the others
_____ Higher than in most of the others
_____ I don't know
_____ About the same as in others
_____ Lower than in most others

17. I feel that I am paid fairly for my work here.

_____ Strongly agree
_____ Agree
_____ Disagree
_____ Strongly disagree
_____ No opinion

18. How well informed are you about policies affecting your pay?

_____ Completely informed
_____ Sufficiently informed
_____ I have some information
_____ I have a little information
_____ I have no idea of the policies

19. How do you rate the granting of pay increases?

_____ Extremely fair
_____ Very fair
_____ Somewhat fair
_____ Not very fair
_____ Not at all fair
_____ I don't know

20. How do you rate your opportunity to earn more money in your present job?

_____ Very good
_____ Good
_____ Adequate
_____ Poor
_____ Very poor

21. I can't complain about the salary increases I have received.

_____ Strongly agree
_____ Agree
_____ Disagree
_____ Strongly disagree
_____ No opinion

22. I understand the reasons for my salary being what it is.

_____ Strongly agree
_____ Agree
_____ Disagree

_____ Strongly disagree
_____ No opinion

F. BENEFITS
23. How do you feel about the following employee benefits?

	Accident Sickness Salary Continuation	*Hospitalization*	*Surgical Care*	*(List additional ones as appropriate)*
I have used it and feel it is adequate	_____	_____	_____	_____
I have used it and feel it is inadequate	_____	_____	_____	_____
I have not used it and feel it is adequate	_____	_____	_____	_____
I have not used it and feel it is inadequate	_____	_____	_____	_____
I don't have enough information	_____	_____	_____	_____

24. How do you feel about the following benefits?

	Retirement Plan	*Vacation Policy*	*Company Holidays*	*Other Benefits*
Excellent	_____	_____	_____	_____
Good	_____	_____	_____	_____

Adequate   _____   _____   _____   _____

Poor   _____   _____   _____   _____

I don't have
enough
information   _____   _____   _____   _____

G.   AUTHORITY/AUTONOMY

25.   How clear are you about the limits of your authority in your present position?

_____ I am very clear

_____ Quite clear on most things

_____ Fairly clear

_____ Not too clear

_____ I am not at all clear

26.   To what extent do you understand the reasoning behind decisions made at higher levels which affect your job?

_____ Very great extent

_____ Great extent

_____ Some extent

_____ Limited extent

_____ Not at all

27.   How often are you bothered by not being able to carry out an assignment because you lack the authority to do so?

_____ Always

_____ Usually

_____ Sometimes

_____ Seldom

_____ Never

28.   In your group, how often are important decisions delayed because someone in management is hesitant to make them?

_____ Always

_____ Usually

_____ Sometimes

_____ Seldom

_____ Never

29.   Too many people have to approve decisions that I make.

_____ Strongly agree

_____ Agree

_____ Disagree

_____ Strongly disagree

_____ No opinion

30. In the past month, how often have you received conflicting orders about your work from different people?

_____ Several times a day

_____ About once a day

_____ Two or three times a week

_____ About once a week

_____ Less than once a month

31. How often are you able to set the completion dates for your jobs?

_____ Almost always

_____ About 75% of the time

_____ About 50% of the time

_____ About 25% of the time

_____ Almost never

32. How much freedom do you have in choosing the jobs on which you work?

_____ I have no choice; I must work on every job assigned to me.

_____ I have some choice; there are a few jobs I can turn down.

_____ I have a lot of choice; there are many jobs which I can turn down.

_____ I have almost complete choice; I work only on jobs I want to.

H. JOB PROGRESS AND CAREER NEEDS

33. How do you feel about the job progress you have made so far?

_____ Much better than I had hoped to make.

_____ Better than I had hoped to make.

_____ As good as I had hoped to make.

_____ Not as good as I had hoped to make.

_____ Much poorer than I had hoped to make.

34. I am pretty well satisfied with the chances of getting ahead in my present work.

_____ Strongly agree

_____ Agree

_____ Disagree

_____ Strongly disagree

_____ Don't know

35. I am fairly confident that my career aspirations can be satis
    fied with my current employer.

    _____ Strongly agree

    _____ Agree

    _____ Disagree

    _____ Strongly disagree

    _____ No opinion

36. I have changed or considered changing my occupational field
    during the last five years.

    _____ Yes

    _____ No

37. There is an occupational field in which I would rather be em-
    ployed than in my present line of work.

    _____ Yes

    _____ No

38. If your answer to the previous question was yes, do you expect
    to be searching for a way to make a career change in the foresee-
    able future?

    _____ Yes

    _____ No

Index

material success, class of '67 and, 65
matrix organization, structure of, 137–141
Mead, Margaret, 55
Meyer, H. H., 88 n., 100 n., 106
Michigan, University of, 88
midcareer crisis, divorce and, 38–39
middle management
  change through, 150–151
  differentiation and integration in, 3–4
  growth of, 2–3
  inequitable salary of, 12–13
  negative attitude toward, 20–21
  rationale for, 2
  responsibility and, 3–4
  special-interest action groups in, 50
  subordinates' views of, 21–24
middle manager(s)
  alcoholism in, 36–38
  alienation of, 48–49
  "boxing in" of, 108–109
  career inflexibility of, 17–18
  change and, 142–144
  coping by, 25–53
  defined, 1–8
  dissatisfaction of, 9–11
  distrust of unions by, 51
  divorce among, 38–39
  effective and ineffective performance by, 146
  empire building by, 35
  frustration and discontent of, 48–49
  functions of, 4–6
  future outlook for, 25
  goal setting and performance review for, 87–107
  group coping by, 42–53
  indecisiveness of, 22
  as individuals, 25–41
  industrial democracy and, 135–137
  inflexibility of, 22
  information technology and, 126–132
  job enrichment for, 111–115
  job insecurity of, 13–14, 18
  lack of authority in, 14–17, 23
  lack of legal protection for, 51
  lack of militancy in, 50–51
  midcareer crisis of, 26–30
  new alternatives for, 108–125
  next generation of, 54–67
  number of, 6–8
  obsolescence of, 18–20
  perceived problems of, 9–24
  perception of, 20–24
  position titles in, 5
  questionnaire survey for, 154–162
  redirection of effort in, 33
  reeducation for, 39–40
  role of in future organization, 126–144
  salary dissatisfaction of, 23
  stagnation of, 28–29
  top management view of, 20–21
  unions and, 42–47
  "unrealistic attitude" of, 20
  upper and lower limits for, 5
midlife crisis, 26–30
Mitbestimmung approach, 135
mobility
  learning-based pay in, 134
  organization or individual initiative in, 30
Moses, as "management consultant," 1–2
Murray, Thomas J., 38, 39 n.
Myers, M. S., 149

National Labor Relations Act, 45
National Council on Alcoholism, 36–38, 41